JAN S

Part 1: Gula

Martin Stepek

Cadzow-Haczow Books

CADZOW-HACZOW BOOKS 2024

Foreword

All Polish words, including names of individuals and places have been spelled using English language letters for ease of publication.

Some place names, especially in Ukraine and the Middle East have proved difficult to locate on modern maps, because many of the original names were changed as and when different political regimes renamed cities, towns, and villages to reflect their own priorities.

I have given some place names multiple spellings, especially in the Middle East, to remain faithful to what the main characters in this book called them, reflecting the chaotic circumstances the Polish people were enduring in those years of wandering whilst seeking refuge and freedom.

Preface

Wladyslaw meets Wladyslaw

As with many memories from long ago, Danka couldn't remember the exact date, or even what season it was, though it wasn't winter. She said she'd have remembered had it been snowing or cold. It was definitely a pleasant day, quite warm.

Why she was in the house that day too, she couldn't remember. It was in her childhood. She knew the year. 1936. She was sure about that because she was eight years old. She must have been told to come in by her mother, because unless she was forced to, she spent her entire childhood out in the fields, up in the trees, swinging from branch to branch, making castles from the mud when it rained. Yes, she must have been told to stay in. Staying in was boring. Staying in was what Zosia did. Zosia was her big sister. She read books.

The only books Danka read were her mum's. They showed which mushrooms you could pick and eat safely, and which ones would kill you. That's a real book, Danka thought.

That's when there was a knock on the door.

A knock on the door? In the few years of life that she had had, or in the years that followed for that matter, she couldn't recollect ever hearing a knock on the door. Visitors always went round to the back of the house to the fields to say hello or would just wave through the window then open the door and say hello.

Danka opened the door. A stranger. That was even more unusual than the knock on the door. She had never seen a stranger at her home before. He was quite old-looking, but to a girl of eight that could mean anything. He was smartly dressed in a jacket and tie but that was not so unusual in those times.

"I'm looking for Wladyslaw Stepek. I was told he lives here."

"Yes he does. I'll go get him. Who shall I say is asking for him?"

"Tell him another Wladyslaw Stepek is here."

Well that was yet another surprise to Danka. She thought she knew all her cousins and uncles.

Danka ran to the fields to fetch her father, who came limping back with her and asked the visitor to come in to the house.

"I hear we share the same name. Wladyslaw Stepek. It's not a common name, except in Haczow where I was born, and that's over a hundred kilometres away."

"I was told to use your name long ago. In Ukraine, near the Sea of Azov. 1915. We were in the prisoner-of-war camp together. You'll surely know now who I am." He smiled.

"Anyway, I was released from Siberia about a year ago, and have been looking for you since then. I wanted to thank you for the name. It saved my life, as you well know."

Part 1

Beginnings

Origins

According to family legend the Stepeks were farmers who had ploughed the same land in Haczow as far back as the 14th century when local records began, and when the village name had not yet existed. Haczow is a small pretty town in the predominantly rural south-eastern tip of Poland. It is less than an hour's drive from Ukraine to the east and Slovakia to the south. A close-knit community of less than two thousand people, it is most famous for its UNESCO World Heritage Site, a gorgeous fifteenth century wooden church, the largest structure of its kind in Europe. That's the church where my ancestors were baptised, married, and where their funerals were held before being buried in the local cemetery.

At the main crossroad in the town stands a monument to those who fought, resisted, and died in the two World Wars. More recently there have been added local victims of oppression from after the Second World War until the fall of communism in Poland in 1989. It features the names of several men called Stepek.

Czeslaw Stepek's name is there. He died a political prisoner at Auschwitz in 1942. Thirteen people from Haczow died in Auschwitz.

A Stanislaw Stepek was killed serving in the Polish resistance. He is remembered on the monument.

Wladyslaw Stepek's name is there. He was my grandfather.

Stepek is a very common name in Haczow and the surrounding towns and villages. But it is not at all common in the rest of Poland or around the world. There are a few Slovaks and Czechs with the name, and of course migrant families like my own have made the name spread as far afield as America and New Zealand. It's a real name, not one of the Polish surnames shortened to be more readily pronounceable by people in other countries. It's pronounced like an amalgamation of the two English words, step and peck, so it's unusually phonetic for a Polish name. Looking at surname maps on the internet the hub and therefore the likely origin of Stepek is still in Haczow.

The beautifully tended village cemetery contains Wladyslaw's grave, giving his year of death as 1943. Inscribed on the same marble stone that marks his burial place are words inscribed by his three children to their mother, his wife, Janina. She is not buried alongside her husband but lies far away in another continent. How this came to pass is at the core of this book.

A family legend states that during one of the many wars or skirmishes between Sweden and Poland a group of Swedish noblemen were captured. Because of their status they were treated with mercy and chivalry. They were given land in Haczow and all that they needed to settle and make prosperous new lives for themselves. Thus according to this story the Stepek lineage is ultimately Swedish, not Polish. However if we look at the main Swedish invasion of Poland as a guideline this would place the arrival of the ancestors of the Stepeks between 1563 and around 1629, three centuries after Haczow was founded. This directly contradicts the story that the Stepeks were there right from the founding of the village. The only evidence, and it is slight, in support of the Swedish legend is that many of the families living in Haczow have blonde or fair hair, which is an unusual feature in Poland.

However, I have had my DNA tested, as have other direct relatives, so we have more to go on than legend and historical events. Most importantly, my Aunt Danka, Maria Danuta Stepek, when tested on Ancestry and My Heritage DNA sites, had Scandinavian ethnicity scores of 13% and 27.5% respectively. Two of my siblings tested on similar sites attained scores of between 4% and 24% under the ethnic group titles Sweden and Denmark or Scandinavia. My own scores in this regard were negligible, however I think that three family members scoring significant percentages of Scandinavian ethnicity in their DNA does give strong credibility to the legend on Haczow's origins.

Researching my heritage, with fantastic help from local people in Haczow, the earliest confirmed ancestor named Stepek is Wojciech (pronounced Voy-check). He was born around 1767 when Poland was still one of the largest countries in Europe. However it was just before the three partitions of the late eighteenth century which wiped Poland off the map of Europe. The Partitions of Poland was a land-grab at Poland's expense by its three imperial neighbours, the Austrian, Prussian and Russian Empires. Thereafter the generations that came lived under Austrian occupation: Mateusz (born 1809), Pawel (born 1839), Jan (born 1869). Both Pawel and Jan died young. Pawel aged just thirty-three, probably of tuberculosis which was one of the major killers until well into the twentieth century. Of course they all married so we have several other named ancestors, all from Haczow. These include Sieniawska, Szuber, Szajna, Jakiel, Rymar, all Haczow names. The Szajnas were sometimes mayors of the town, as were some other relatives but as Haczow is so small, probably every family has such "noble" ancestry. All these ancestors were born, lived and died in Haczow but that is all we know about them. To get to know the life of one of my Stepek ancestors we must start in 1893 with Wladyslaw, my grandfather.

Wladyslaw

Wladyslaw Stepek was born on 19 September 1893 in a wooden bungalow on the outskirts of the village, with farming land behind it. The house is believed to have been built some time before 1800 and is made of very thick long logs. It remains in family hands. Even today it looks like it could last a thousand years and remains striking and almost new thanks to painstaking maintenance and paintwork. It resembles a log cabin, only bigger and sturdier.

Wladyslaw's parents were Jan Stepek and Aniela Sieniawska. Jan was only thirty-nine when he died in 1908, Aniela forty, in 1913. So Wladyslaw was fourteen when his father died, and nineteen when his mother died.

Wladyslaw too nearly died young, of tuberculosis, when he was a child but he was lucky and survived. Many of his siblings would not be so lucky. Wladyslaw was the first-born, then followed:

Stanislaw 8-12-95 to 18-8-1926 Died age 30 years. (Emigrated to USA in 1913 where he died)

Marianna 13-9-97 to 3-10-97 Died age 20 days

Jozef 5-11-98 to 28-11-98 Died age 23 days

Helena 7-1-1900 to 9-12-1987 Died age 87 years

Ignacy 28-4-01 to 1-6-02 Died aged 13 months

Anna 11-1-04 to 13-1-04 Died age 2 days

Aleksandra 23-11-06 to 2-11-88 Died age 81 years

Marianna 1-8-07 to 16-6-08 Died age 10 months

In a farming family Wladyslaw would have learned through experience how to manage the fields and was an adult by the time his mother died. Stanislaw his younger brother was only two years younger so he too would have helped keep the farm until he emigrated to the USA.

The two sisters who survived childhood, Helena and Aleksandra, were only thirteen and six years old respectively when orphaned so we understand that the two girls were taken in by relatives. It's not known whether relatives or Godparents took both, or if they were housed in different homes. Regardless, Haczow was a very small, safe rural village so the four children would have remained in daily touch with one another.

These two sisters later lived together in the family home in Haczow until they both died in the 1980s, and throughout that period they tended the land together.

At the time of Wladyslaw's birth Poland had endured almost a century of occupation under its three neighbouring empires. Despite numerous failed uprisings the Polish people seemed destined always to live under foreign rule. The memory of their country's past triumphs and significance in Europe seemed fated to fade into distant history.

Austria, which controlled the region named Galicia which Haczow was part of, was a relatively benign force in the late nineteenth and early twentieth century compared to the other two imperial powers that controlled Poland.

Wladyslaw was well educated. He had completed six years of high school in nearby Sanok by around 1910. He then left Haczow at the age of eighteen and went to Strumien, in the south-west of present-day Poland, to practise as a pharmacist. Family lore has it that he took a degree in pharmacy at the University of Lwow, or Jagiellonian University in Krakow or at Vienna but there is no proof of this as yet. In Strumien an experienced pharmacist was already well-known and was called Jan Stepek, so whether Wladyslaw was able to undergo an apprenticeship there with a distant relative, or whether it was just a coincidence, we don't know.

Despite the loss of their brothers and sisters, then their parents, life was looking good for the young siblings as they grew towards adulthood. Educated, with their own farm and a sturdy home, Poland, if not the world was their oyster. For Stanislaw however the lure of America proved too much and he emigrated there in 1913. For the others, theirs was not a peasant life; rather a middling, comfortable existence in a quiet peaceful corner of Europe. Haczow was in fact at that time among the wealthiest areas of what is now Poland.

All that changed in the summer of 1914 when war erupted in Europe. Wladyslaw was twenty, and was soon conscripted into the Austrian army. He was posted to the medical corps because of his experience as a pharmacist. With his sisters being just fourteen and seven, a neighbour was given stewardship of the land in Wladyslaw's absence.

On the 5th April 1915 Wladyslaw was captured by the Russian army in the region of the Carpathian Mountains and initially interred at Kozhukhov in the south of central Ukraine, midway between Lviv and Kyiv. From there he was taken to a prisoner of war camp in southern Ukraine where he was made to work as an assistant chemist in a factory in Stantsiya Sartana near Mariupol at the Azov Sea. We don't know the details of this factory's work but it seems logical to think it was either for the production of essentials for Russian people and society, or was connected to arms production.

Whilst at the factory Wladyslaw spoke to his fellow workers and agitated against the Czar and the Russian occupation of Ukraine and Poland. The authorities soon found out. He was placed in an underground cell whilst the officers in charge considered what to do with him. They sent him to a holding place Wladyslaw later referred to as Barmuta, which may have been in Belarus, to await his punishment. Eventually the news came to him. He had been sentenced to fifteen years in Siberia and paperwork was accordingly drawn up for his long journey into deeper exile from his homeland.

Then fate intervened. He fell ill with tuberculosis for the second time in his life. For some reason the prison camp authorities decided they would operate and see if they could save him. They cut out the infected part of his lung. He was just twenty-one years old. It is hard to contemplate the conditions in which such an operation was undertaken, in a prisoner of war camp in the early part of the twentieth century. Yet somehow he survived, perhaps because of his youthful energy, though it left him with physical disabilities for the rest of his life.

Still, he was to go to Siberia once he recovered and surely in his weakened state that would kill him off. Wladyslaw managed to avoid this fate in a most extraordinary way. He was on good terms with the prison guards while recovering from his lung operation. They regularly played cards together to pass the time whilst the bureaucracy formalised his transfer documents. Wladyslaw was a very good card player and in one game won a lot of money from the guards. The guards however were unable to pay him, presumably because the Russian government was, by this stage of the war, struggling to survive. Wladyslaw suggested that they find a way to give him some stay of execution in exchange for the debt they owed him.

The guards came up with the following plan. They would send another prisoner to Siberia in Wladyslaw's name. A prisoner in the camp had been sentenced to death for attempting to escape and was due to be hanged in the days to come. Given the option this prisoner readily accepted the Siberia sentence along with Wladyslaw's name; a slight chance of survival being much better than no chance.

To cover up the switch in identities they had to fake a hanging so that it looked like the man who had tried to escape was in fact hanged. So they took the body of a third prisoner, who had that day died of natural causes in his cell and was already in a makeshift wooden coffin ready for burial. The guards took his body out of the coffin and hanged it on the gallows. Thus the hanging had taken place.

Finally to complete the circle the guards had to be seen to bury the coffin with the dead man inside it. But when the coffin was actually lowered in the ground it contained no corpse, probably only soil, turf and stones.

The Russian guards wrote up a faithful record of the fate of three of their prisoners:

Wladyslaw Stepek was sent to Siberia;

A would-be absconder was hanged;

and a man who died in the cells was buried in his coffin.

The real Wladyslaw Stepek was sent under an assumed name to a more open prisoner of war camp in the town of Pereslawl-Zalesski, ninety miles north of Moscow (and over eight hundred miles from where he was previously imprisoned), arriving there on 24th March 1916.

According to the archived records Wladyslaw was freed and returned to Austrian hands on 2nd March 1917. We don't know the reason why, but can speculate it was because of his continued ill-health related to tuberculosis and the operation to remove the infected part of his lung.

Back in Haczow Wladyslaw was treated for continued after-effects of his tuberculosis, then was sent to a hospital in Lesa Wielenski, also in Austrian-occupied Poland. He was still officially in the Austrian medical corps but avoided further military action.

Finally in 1918 he was well enough to return to Haczow and was granted unlimited sick leave from the army. Brought up in a radical household and an instinctive fighter for Polish independence, Wladyslaw engaged in political agitation against Austrian rule. He had clearly not learned the lessons of his previous few years.

Again he was arrested, this time sentenced to a short spell in prison, at Przemysl, a major town not far from Haczow. On his release he returned to Haczow, where in the latter half of 1918 he resumed his revolutionary activities. He convinced one hundred and seventy local men to desert the Austrian army and plan for the long-awaited Polish uprising.

This group made contact with the Polish underground army that had been forming to strike for independence as the First World War neared its end. The occupying Austrians were by now a totally exhausted force, and their troops remained in barracks demoralised and disorganised. They were a major weak link in the fragmenting foreign domination of Poland.

Wladyslaw seemed to thrive on risk and adventure. He loved political debate and was infamous locally for his fiery provocative speeches. In 1918 he gave an impromptu eulogy in Haczow cemetery at the burial of a local Polish patriot who had been shot by the Austrian forces. Wladyslaw denounced Austrian rule and urged those present to rise against the wearied Austrian troops. Having already experienced imprisonment by both Russian and Austrian forces, he well knew the potential consequences of such actions. It was no surprise when Austrian soldiers started to move in on him amongst the crowd of mourners at the graveside. The local women crowded together surrounding Wladyslaw, hiding him from the troops and he managed to slip away and evade capture.

Soon after this, he received instructions from the regional division of the underground army. Wladyslaw was to lead a local insurrection and attempt to overcome and disarm the nearby Austrian army garrison at Nohermerjew. This he and his men successfully accomplished on 30th October 1918.

The following month the war ended. Armistice Day was declared across Europe on 11th November 1918. That same day Marshall Jozef Pilsudski declared Poland an independent country again after one hundred and eleven years of occupation. However, despite the collapse of the three imperial forces which had partitioned Poland in 1795, Poland's frontiers were disputed by all its neighbouring countries, and its very existence not secured. Even within the new state many of its minority groups were not supportive of the newly-regained independent Poland. Germans in the previously German-occupied part of the country did not want to be ruled by Poland, and to the east Ukrainian people wanted their own independence.

Wladyslaw volunteered to join the Polish forces under Captain Stanislaw Maczek, (later to become General Maczek, head of the Polish land forces during the Second World War). Wladyslaw brought Maczek one hundred recruits from Haczow. They were immediately sent to fight at the eastern front to combat both the Russian Bolshevik army and

Ukrainian militias, who were determined to prevent the Poles from claiming Western Ukraine as part of Poland.

Ukrainian political and military groups had been planning a military campaign to bring independence to Ukraine, so the situation now became very complicated. Not only were there three national claimants for the same territory, but politically each claimant had different visions for the territory. From a Russian viewpoint the Bolsheviks under Lenin were still seeking to consolidate their October 1917 Revolution, fighting the remnants of the old regime who had not accepted that they had lost the post-revolution civil war in Russia.

The Poles meanwhile had two opposite political leaders. Josef Pilsudski, socialist, Lithuanian by birth, had a vision of a Pan-Slavic Commonwealth of Poland, Ukraine, Belarus, and Lithuania, combining their strengths to stop the Russians from pushing their revolution westwards into the rest of Europe. Roman Dmowski on the other hand, feared German power more, and was willing to reach a compromise with the Russians. His right-wing nationalist vision had no room for those who were not ethnically Polish in the new republic. This latter ideology was particularly threatening for the region's sizeable Jewish community.

Ukrainians were divided into even more radically opposed groups. A pro-Russian, pro-Bolshevik faction; a pro-Polish group; a group which wanted nothing to do with either neighbouring force and sought to gain independence for

Ukraine; and the radical anarchist force under the charismatic Nestor Makhno which sought to consolidate a revolutionary anarchist area in southern Ukraine.

Eventually, after a series of campaigns the Poles secured victory over the Bolshevik forces and negotiated its eastern borders with the Russian revolutionary government. However, although this ended the military campaigns in the east, many on the Russian and Ukrainian sides were enraged at the outcome and refused to accept it as a settled matter.

Looking back, an improbable series of events had conspired to bring the opportunity of freedom and independence to Poland. Few would have predicted the main factors involved. Russia had erupted in two revolutions in February and October 1917. The following year whilst Russia was enmeshed in civil war between Lenin's Bolsheviks and those loyal to the old regime, the war turned against Germany and her ally Austria. Peace was declared on 11 November 1918. The three empires that had partitioned Poland in 1795 and wiped its name off the map of Europe had all in turn been vanquished. Into the vacuum swept Polish officers and troops from all three imperial armies under the leadership of Pilsudksi. Poland existed as a country once again. If it had been suggested as a plot for a novel it would have been rejected as too implausible.

Wladyslaw's political ideology and military activities fitted in seamlessly with this seismic geopolitical shift. He had become known for reckless adventurism and his reputation had grown locally as a young romantic hero who fought and risked his life for the freedom of Poland. This made an impression on one naïve and innocent eighteen year old woman whose family had not many years earlier moved into a village near Haczow.

Janina

Janina Ciupka was born in the family home on a wealthy estate a few miles outside Nieszawa on the River Vistula on the 5th August 1902. Nieszawa is a small town south of Torun and less than one hundred miles north-west of Warsaw. It has a population of around two thousand. The region was under German rule when Janina was born but the family prospered despite or possibly because of this. The family home had two storeys, a grand house which comfortably fitted the large family and their many servants and nannies.

The wider Ciupka clan had enormous families. They were business people and merchants, originally from the city of Gliwice in Upper Silesia, south-west Poland, and seemed to breed ten to eighteen children each as a matter of course. They were well educated by Polish standards at the beginning of the twentieth century. Janina's parents Jozef and Joanna, (maiden name Kozlowska) had a spectacular house when they lived in Gliwice in the years before Janina was born. It had three dining rooms: one for the smaller children, one for the teenage children, and one for the adults. When they moved to Nieszawa around the turn of the century they were breeding rare white horses for pulling carriages that typically required four to six horses. The Russian royal family were among their customers. They kept their core milling business in family hands back in Silesia, and this continued to trade with Czech and Russian merchants whilst Jozef diversified into new forms of business in Nieszawa.

We know of a partial demise of the Ciupka fortune as a result of extravagant endowments to the next generation, and apparently a poor business decision made by Jozef, in buying an estate in Warsaw which he did not know was already mortgaged by another property owner. He lost this property and the money he paid for it, which was substantial. Yet despite the ups and downs in their business dealings they remained a wealthy family.

Janina was the youngest of nine children who survived infancy out of a total of twelve born. One of her four surviving brothers, Jan, drowned in later childhood while he played in the River Vistula. This left eight children who reached adulthood: Sisters Helena, Maria, Lucyna, Irena, and Janina; and three brothers Czeslaw, Henryk and Waclaw, the twin of Jan, the young boy who drowned.

Janina and her three remaining brothers and four sisters lived very privileged lives. The household had several maids. This included personal servants for each of the children who were sheltered from the harsh realities of ordinary people's lives. Servants would take Janina and her friends boating along the River Vistula. The girls would catch lobsters in their nets whilst the servants lit the river by holding out lamps over the sides of the boats.

Janina was being prepared for the life of a lady with no need to learn how to do basic housework, manual labour or the sweat and toil that was the daily experience of most of her fellow Poles. However not even the most protective of environments can guarantee safety. In her early teenage years she had to have her right thumb amputated as a result of a bad fall from her horse. Fortunately she was left-handed so was able to adapt to a great extent despite this disability.

She was educated at home by teachers and a private governess, in part because the German rulers had passed laws decreeing that Polish language, Polish literature and Polish history could not be taught in schools.

The three boys went to the prestigious Jagiellonian University in Krakow, one of Europe's oldest universities, founded in 1364. Women were still not permitted to go to university at that time. This was a great irony as the remarkable Polish scientist Maria Sklodowska, better known as Marie Curie, was at that time winning not one but two Nobel Prizes in the first decade of Janina's life. Instead Janina and her sisters were sent to that quaintly termed European institution, a ladies' finishing school.

According to family stories, relations between Germans and Poles in the region, which were already tense, took a turn for the worse. One of their rich German neighbours became abusive and aggressive towards the family. In 1909 Jozef decided the situation was too unpleasant for his family so he sold his successful granary and mill business in Silesia and bought an estate in Austrian-occupied Poland where he set up another corn-milling business in a village called Wroblik Krolewski – which means Royal Sparrow - just a kilometre or so from Haczow. Sadly the mill no longer exists. It was burned down during the Second World War.

Here Jozef felt his family would be safer from German aggression and the Germans could not conscript his sons into their notoriously harsh army regime. Life under Austrian rule was generally more liberal and less severe for Poles than under the Germans or Russians. Locally there were high calibre private schools for the younger children. Janina was seven years old when they moved and was enrolled in a convent school for girls from the elite of Poland's families.

Janina's elder brothers became involved in various businesses: engineering, transportation, and brickmaking. The remains of the Ciupka brickworks in Wroblik Krolewski still exists. They were a versatile and entrepreneurial family. Janina's elder sister Maria married into the noble Konopnicki family, who had an estate in south-east Poland which was part of the wider family lands.

At the outset of the First World War Janina's brothers were conscripted to the Austrian army but in due course they deserted to join the underground army preparing for independence for Poland. It is conceivable that it was Wladyslaw who persuaded them to desert and join his volunteer unit, and that this turn of events would later lead to Janina's brothers introducing Wladyslaw to Janina.

After she graduated from high school it was intended that she would go to Vienna for a year at finishing school. It is unknown if she ever did this final year. Janina's daughter, Zosia believes that she did, and that Janina had just left finishing school when she met Wladyslaw. It's not certain when the two met but the most likely guess would be early in 1920.

Their romance reads like a Mills and Boon parody. Janina the rich society girl, used to being waited on hand and foot, meets and falls in love with the semi-invalided activist and revolutionary local war hero who defeated the Austrians in their own garrison. It was not a very practical combination; a war hero who was a small landowner but who didn't really know how to make the most of the potential of the farm; and a lady of leisure who knew very little about real life. But love is blind and the two romantics decided to forge a life together amidst the ruins and economic chaos of post-war Europe.

Marriage and a Fateful Decision

The young couple married on 26th November 1921. Janina was only nineteen, Wladyslaw almost ten years older.

Almost a year earlier, on 17th of December 1920 the Polish Parliament passed an act granting land to ex-military personnel. The land was in the newly regained eastern regions of Poland, the areas that bordered communist Russia. This region was still considered vulnerable to attack from Russia or from militants amongst the Ukrainian people who lived there. Before the partitions in the eighteenth century these lands had been ruled over by the Commonwealth of Lithuania-Poland but had most recently been under Russian rule for over a hundred years. Matters were even more complicated. Ukrainians had sought unsuccessfully to win their own independence, through both military and political means. So too had Belarusians and Lithuanians, all in this area seized by Poland. From the Polish government's perspective it made sense to fortify the border areas known as the Kresy with vibrant but hardened young war veterans and their new wives. They would be instructed to build a network of small new settlements. From many Ukrainians' point of view however, this looked like just another wave of imperial settlers, symbolising the oppression of their own desire for independence, and therefore something to be opposed, within new political structures, or through violent struggle.

Poland had trouble with all of its neighbours as all of the border regions were disputed. In the spring of 1921 a major uprising erupted at Poland's south-western border. It was in the region of Górny Śląsk where the territory was disputed primarily between Germany and Poland. It was made subject to a referendum by the recently created League of Nations but both sides increased militant activity in the area in the lead up to the vote. On 11th May Wladyslaw volunteered at the city of Lwów to join the forces fighting to ensure the region was made part of Poland. He was accepted but in the end was not required to be sent to the front. His efforts expended, he returned to Haczów to prepare to marry his young fiancée.

When they married in 1921 they initially lived in the Stepek farmhouse in Haczów sharing it with Wladyslaw's two sisters Helena and Aleksandra. Life became very uncomfortable for young Janina. She had had no experience of domestic or farm work and Wladyslaw's sisters were very unhappy about what they considered Janina's sheer lack of competence. They were born farmers, mucking out barns and doing physical labour in the fields from their early years. They were also orphans, used to just getting on with life's ups and downs, as well as the arduous daily housework.

Perhaps it was as a result of this unhappy atmosphere in the house, and his sense of sympathy for his young wife that Wladyslaw took up the offer to move east that year and take advantage of the grants of land there. The other motive was his sense of patriotic duty, even the chance of more military adventure. Whatever the reasons the decision was made to accept a plot of land to add to his family's farming assets. Wladyslaw returned the management of the Haczów farm to Helena and Aleksandra while he and Janina looked forward to settling on the lush lands of the west of Ukraine. The young couple now owned two farms and life looked very promising.

Part 2: Maczkowce

Building a Home in a Divided Community

The move to Ukraine, either in the autumn of 1921 or the spring of 1922 had an ominous beginning. One of their wedding presents was a beautiful set of expensive china. During the 150-mile journey from Haczów to their new farmland a cart containing the precious china overturned and only a few plates survived. Their younger daughter Danka recollected that the china was so fine it was translucent but quickly added that such fine plates weren't exactly suitable for life on a farm. By this time Janina was possibly in the early stages of her first pregnancy, though she may not have known this at the time of the departure to their new home.

The part of today's Ukraine which was to be their new home looked like the rolling forested counties of Ayrshire and Perthshire in Scotland with rich fertile valleys where almost any crop could flourish. The soil was up to seven metres in depth having been deposited by glaciers then rivers which had carved out the valleys. It was said that you could drop a seed into the soil and watch it grow. In spring wild cherry trees blossomed as if overnight and the whole valley awoke, filled with beautiful flowers and scents. There were wolves, hares, wild goats and boars. But the new settlers were not hunters; their priority was to plough the land which, because of the

First World War then the consequent Polish-Russian war, had lain not only uncultivated, but obliterated for more than six years.

The land was twenty-five kilometres south of Luck, a city of around 200,000 people, now called Lutsk in western Ukraine. The estate which they had been given was known as Jezierany Uroczysko, which means "pretty lake district." The settlers were told that it had once belonged to a Polish nobleman. It is said that he had been sent to Siberia for his support of the Polish insurrection against Russian occupation in 1831. The estate was then granted by the Czar to a Russian General called Bielajew as a reward for his efforts in crushing the Polish insurrection. After the second Russian Revolution of 1917 the descendants of the General disappeared. The most accepted local story was that they were murdered by the Bolsheviks, but another version suggested that they had escaped into exile in France.

All these stories must be taken with a pinch of salt. The whole topic of sovereignty and land ownership was politically and ideologically charged, so the story that this land was originally taken from Polish hands helped justify the plantation of Polish military settlers in the Kresy region. Undoubtedly the local Ukrainians and the Bolshevik Russians had different versions of past ownership of the estate, or a different perspective of the history. I have found no evidence to support any version of these stories.

The nearest village was Jeziorany. It consisted of a score or so farms and a few more homes. Kolonia, a few kilometres away, was said to have been created as dwelling places for the servants who worked for the Polish nobleman who founded and lived in the estate.

The estate home was still fully intact when the new Polish families arrived. Hundreds of years old, it was made of wood, and had more than ten rooms plus stables and outhouses, all on one floor. Somehow it had survived all the wars and insurrections over the past two centuries. When the young settler couples first arrived they all stayed together in this large manor house. They moved out one couple at a time as each new home was built by communal labour, helped by some funding from central government. Each new home was different from the rest, reflecting their own aesthetic tastes.

There were twenty-three couples in the original settlement, which comprised a total of 362 hectares of prime farming land. Most had come from Haczow. Eventually all twenty-three had their homes built. The community was then granted additional land; the adjacent forested area called Korczunk, which allowed another five families to build homes in that area. The nearest river was twenty kilometres away and flowed all the way to the Black Sea. The first summer was typical of the years to come; summers were warm and dry while winters were harsh, with minus ten degrees centigrade on an average winter's day, occasionally falling to minus fifteen. In extreme years the temperature dropped below minus thirty.

In 1924 the community named the settlement Maczkowce in honour of Captain Stanisław Maczek who had led the settlers' menfolk in their military exploits from late 1918 through to 1920. They were all young men and women in their twenties, and the men brought with them their war-time weaponry for the defence of their homes and the border area. The nearest town with shops was Boreml, about fifteen kilometres away. There were two railway stations within walking distance, and the nearest church was six kilometres away. On the few occasions when the family went into town they would go by horse and cart, otherwise on horseback or walking was the dominant method of getting around.

The new Stepek farmhouse was built on the southernmost one of two gently rising slopes on the farm, about two hundred yards from the valley floor. Down the hill from the farmhouse on its right-hand side, Wladyslaw planted and grew an orchard. Further down the small valley between the two slopes snow would build up over the winter. When it finally thawed it became a temporary stream then a pond until late spring when it dried out.

To the left of the house was a well, which had plentiful amounts of water all year round. Standing near it you could hear the gurgle of the underground stream that flowed ten metres below ground level. The well wall was made of concrete on top of a limestone base and water was drawn from the well using the traditional bucket on a pulley rope.

Janina had been given a large dowry when she married. Wladyslaw spent much of this on his new neighbours, most of whom had been friends in his military adventures. He gave them funds with which to build their new homes in the settlement. He was repaid in labour and bricks. Soon new buildings were built on the Stepek farm and these developments continued throughout the seventeen years from 1922 to 1939. The final stages of the family's farming plans were never completed because of the onset of the Second World War, but by then the family lived in a comfortable home with outbuildings where corn was kept both for livestock and for the family. Wladyslaw was very friendly towards people, both in the original settlement and to those in the neighbouring villages. He would give easily, and as he had an unusually positive view of a multi-cultural Poland he became popular with local people of the various different ethnic groups. He travelled widely in the area on their behalf, despite the burden of his poor health.

Their home was close to the mid-point of the settlement of farms with one neighbour nearby across the main road. Their nearest neighbours to either side of them were each around half a kilometre away to the north and south. The farm also stretched half a kilometre to the east and half a kilometre to the west. One of their neighbours still lived in the original estate home. To travel from one end of the settlement to the other was around ten kilometres.

The first home the Stepeks built was a simple construction with floors made of a mud-straw mix rather than wooden floors as it was dry in the Ukraine. They had chimneys and a simple but effective central heating system. Jan remembers a flat iron roof but Danka thinks that the roof had large slates. Perhaps, being the eldest, Jan remembers the original roof which may have been replaced later. The house itself was made of wood, a bungalow like a cabin. Eventually the family home had three rooms adjoined directly by the byre which housed pigs and cattle, and a stable for the family's four horses. This meant they didn't have to leave the house to attend to the animals in winter and all of the heat was retained in the house. Unfortunately it also meant that they could hear and smell the animals from the house.

However at the beginning when Jan was a very young boy in the early to mid 1920s the house comprised just the living room, where they also slept, and the kitchen. All the children remember that the kitchen had an oven in which their mother regularly baked bread. In later years at wintertime the girls used to climb above it to feel snug and warm.

The toilet was outside and all water had to be fetched from the well. This was particularly unpleasant in winter when it was so cold that ice formed all around the building. Moreover heavy buckets of water had to be carried in for the animals as well as the family.

Because he was a pharmacist people used to come to Wladyslaw at the farm to write them prescriptions, which had to be done in Latin. Zosia thinks Wladyslaw must have studied at post-graduate level after the First World War to become a qualified pharmacist but there is no evidence for this as yet. Perhaps as Poland was still trying to rebuild its society after a century of being partitioned such qualifications may have been considered an unnecessary luxury.

Wladyslaw also wrote letters for local people who came to him, directed to local authorities or employers regarding the state of the individual's health. Both Wladyslaw and Janina were well educated, which was unusual in the eastern borders area. Even Janina's best friend was unable to sign her own name despite coming from a noble family, so illiteracy was common.

Wladyslaw saw the venture to build a new community as a utopian vision, but Janina was completely unprepared for the scale of the task they had undertaken. They had to build their own home and help build all the other homes in the settlement. She was a young woman who had always had servants to do everything for her. It must have been like those old western movies from America, where the lady appears, dressed in fashionable European clothes, stepping off the stagecoach, from an east coast city to a dusty, pioneering wild west town of rough cowboys and dangerous gunslingers.

This was the initial impression the children had of their mother. But although this may have been true of her early years in the farm, she came to play a significant role in the community. At home she did a lot of baking and was a very good cook. She was caring and protective about what Jan wore, that he should be warm enough when he ventured outdoors especially in winter. Jan typically wouldn't wear an overcoat and refused to go to school when she made him wear a scarf.

To prove to herself and others that she could learn to make a meaningful contribution to the community Janina undertook a course on different species of trees for orchards. The trees covered in the course were available from Austria. She then set about organising the local women. She started sewing and cooking classes and galvanised practical activity amongst the womenfolk.

Wladyslaw remained a political and community leader. He organised the Youth Strzelec, or riflemen, a military organisation that Marshall Pilsudski had set up for young people, akin to the Scout movement, but with weapons. It was taken seriously as an organisation because in Poland there was always a tangible fear of invasion from the east or west. Training involved cavalry exercises and shooting practice for young cadets. Wladyslaw ran the local branch of this organisation, which held regular activities involving all the nearby villages. Therefore as one might expect, in 1933, at the age of eleven, Jan and other local Polish children were taught by Wladyslaw how to use a rifle. This was primarily so they could defend themselves against militant Ukrainian nationalists from whom there was a constant threat of violence by the 1930s. These minority groups supported the violent route to Ukrainian independence and would make night-time raids on villages and attempt to burn down one or more of the houses owned by ethnic Poles. Jan recalls seeing houses burning in the distance and hearing shooting in the night but no one he knew was killed. The military settlers of Maczkowce were surrounded by Ukrainian villages and to Jan it felt a bit like living in the Wild West.

There was a lot of singing at home and at school. Both parents had good voices and taught music to the local children but Jan was always told not to join in because he couldn't sing in tune. During the long period of the Russian Partition education of Polish language, history and culture was forbidden even to the ethnic Poles living there, so Wladyslaw taught local villagers Polish history and folk songs. He went to the nearest city, Luck, repeatedly to argue for more teachers to be sent to the area. Eventually he succeeded. Taking the initiative, he brought one teacher all the way from Krakow to found a new school which the community built from scratch in 1934. The school started with just one class in the morning then grew to two classes in the morning, and then eventually two more in the afternoon.

Wladyslaw's and Janina's industry and passion were impressive. They started a local library in a community hall next to the village school. The hall also served as a dance hall, a meeting room, and the place where the local Christmas party was held each year. Wladyslaw suggested and oversaw the creation of a creamery to separate cream from milk, from which butter was then produced for local consumption. This entrepreneurial idea came in response to a glut of milk being produced locally. So much milk was being produced that it more than met the demand from local people. Even the pigs were fed cows' milk, and few local people bought milk because most had their own cow or could barter what they grew for neighbours' milk.

Wladyslaw started plans to build a church in Maczkowce. The location was chosen and had been given permission from the Catholic Church and local government. Building was due to start in 1940 but by then war had broken out.

Children from three other villages - Ukrainian, Czech and German – came to the new local school. Quite a lot of the Ukrainian children were poor, living on small peasant farms which barely produced enough food for the family to survive. Janina organised what was called "second breakfast", whereby each of the Polish families' mothers would take it in turn to ensure that these children were fed. The usual fare included ham sandwiches, cheese sandwiches, butter and milk.

Wladyslaw had plans to eventually work in a pharmacy in Łuck. By the late 1930s he was authorised to diagnose people's illnesses after consultation with them. People started to come to the house from far and wide asking Wladyslaw to write letters for them, often asking him to write in German because they wanted to contact family members in Germany or Austria. Another common request was for Wladyslaw to draft letters complaining about the level of taxes being demanded by local or national government and giving reasons why these should be reduced. As a result the regional civil servants came to know Wladyslaw well, and recognised that he had good knowledge of the law. He was not afraid to stand up against the authorities, for whom he had scant respect as the Polish military regime had become more and more right-wing and autocratic through the 1930s.

Wladyslaw and Janina's community spirit was probably typical of many in the twenty-one years of the Second Republic. Having regained independence after one hundred and twenty-three years of being oppressed by neighbouring empires there was a mood amongst Poles to rebuild their shattered country. They wanted to show the wider world that Poland could be a powerful, wealthy, successful modern state. France in particular was viewed by educated Poles as a role model of a cultured, democratic country.

In Polish villages people were filled with this spirit of national renewal and their children soaked in every drop of this mood. Patriotism, with all its positive and negative qualities, was in the air of every Polish home and it was reflected in the pride they took in building unique homes, in striving to make agriculture more effective, and in bringing higher levels of education to their children. This was certainly the case in the small community of Maczkowce where every man who founded the settlement had fought for Poland's independence from 1918 to 1920 so their resolve was intense.

However one group's patriotism is another's reason to fear and hate. Not everyone in Poland shared the same vision for the country nor the same outlook. This newly reborn Poland was a deeply complex, multi-cultural society with many competing nationalist and ethnic visions. Roughly ten percent of the population, much higher in the east, was Ukrainian, and they had sought the establishment of their own independent state at the Versailles talks which were held to redraw the map of Europe in the aftermath of the 1914-18 war.

The Jewish people of Poland also made up roughly ten percent of the total Polish population, again higher in the east where the Stepeks settled. Jews had lived in Poland for a thousand years, and grew in numbers over the centuries pushed by expulsions from other European countries. They were also drawn by guarantees by the Polish-Lithuanian rulers that their faith, liberty and trade would be safeguarded.

During the period of the Partitions of Poland, however, ruthless pogroms and mistreatment made many Jews fearful and wary of any government that ruled over them. By the time Poland regained its independence an enormous amount of damage had been done. Assimilation was very limited; a census in the 1930s showed that almost 80% of Polish Jews spoke only Yiddish, which clearly had major implications for communication with the various other peoples of the country.

Moreover Zionism, the movement for an independent Jewish state, had developed as a concept in the nineteenth century. By the time Poland had regained its independence this vision of a Jewish homeland had been formally supported by the then world's most powerful nation, Great Britain. Thus for many Jews in Poland, as in the rest of Europe, around the Middle East, and in America there was a tantalising vision which competed for their loyalty and energy with the country in which they were living. Added to this were the toxic antisemitic policies of some major right wing political parties in Poland, exacerbated by relentless propaganda and misinformation deliberately directed towards the country by neighbouring Nazi-governed Germany from 1933 onwards. This led to growing antisemitic actions by the Polish government in the late nineteen thirties.

However, locally there appeared to be few tensions or problems between ethnic Poles and Jews in the villages and towns around Maczkowce. Friendly interaction between Jews and Poles and the other ethnic groups in the area existed right from the start of the new Maczkowce community.

There were many Jewish families living in the area, the nearest being a large community who stayed in a German-dominated village. The Jews didn't work on the land but rather went from farm to farm trading goods for wheat or fruit. In the nearest city, Luck, Jews comprised almost half of the total population. Jan occasionally went to this city with his father and passed through the Jewish quarter to get to the city centre. He remembers the Jewish quarter smelling sweetly of fruit and strongly of fish. His memory of the Jews in the region was that both those in the city and the ones living nearer the farms were poor.

In Poland there was also a large German population, again almost ten percent of the population, which had grown over the century that first Prussia then Germany controlled north-west Poland. Most of these supported German claims on the land that was taken in the west by Poland after the First World War.

In addition to these major national and cultural differences there were four powerful ideological forces at play during this period. The extreme political ideologies of Fascism and Communism increasingly seeped into Poland through propaganda by both Nazi Germany and Stalin's Soviet Union, with supporters of both these views active in Poland. Over and above this was the growth of nationalism in the hearts and minds of all the ethnic groups in the country – the Poles, Ukrainians, Jews, and Germans being the largest groupings, but which also included smaller but still significant numbers of Czechs, Slovaks, Russians, Belarussians, and Lithuanians, all of whom had deep attachment to their own national heritage and traditional homelands. Finally the historical partitions of Poland meant that for over a century people in various groups believed that certain regions ought to have remained German, Russian or Austrian. So the Poland that the Stepeks grew up and lived in was a hugely complex mix of competing nationalisms, ideologies and radically differing views of history.

These tensions played out in the education system locally. The settlement's school was built near the Stepek home on land left by a man who had been given the largest part of the estate alongside some common land. Jan was the only one of the three Stepek children to go to a different local school because he had finished primary education before the Maczkowce school was built.

People looked up to Wladyslaw because he had done so much, particularly in his role organising military youth from the age of fifteen to fight for Poland's defence. But his forthright style and sharp tongue made many enemies in dangerous quarters. He wasn't afraid to stir things up, never going along with official directives if he disagreed with them, and it was in his nature to dispute many of the military regime's increasingly extreme policies.

Many Ukrainian activists were reluctant to work with the Poles because they felt they would never get their own way as they were the minority group. Wladyslaw had a different ideology, based on Jozef Pilsudski's original vision of a commonwealth between Poles, Ukrainians and Lithuanians. Wladyslaw helped Ukrainians with their problems, and tried to reconcile Ukrainians and Poles who were in dispute with one another. Local Ukrainian militants were angered by this as they felt their separatist vision was challenged by these examples of working collaboration and partnership.

In spite of this hostility and distrust Wladyslaw continued to act as an arbitrator for Ukrainians in land disputes, which were common. He wrote letters for them to the courts and guided them through law relating to land ownership. More and more of them came to the house for advice. In his spare time he started researching their names and discovered that some of them came from Polish families. Their names had been Russified during the partitions under Catherine the Great when all things Polish were oppressed and persecuted. Looking further he found many of the local people's ancestral graves. These bore the families' original Polish names but many of the local people were illiterate and many of the older Polish graves were in Latin script rather than the Cyrillic script used in Ukrainian. Thus some were unsure whether

Wladyslaw was telling them the truth or not. It is estimated that he convinced around three hundred local people to convert to Catholicism by showing them evidence of their Polish ancestry. This work further angered the militant Ukrainian nationalists who saw Wladyslaw's actions in this area as anti-Ukrainian, pro-Polish propaganda and a decision was reached that he had to be killed in order to stop his activities.

This was no idle threat as other people in the area had been shot as they sat at their window at night. There were not many deaths but they made a great impact and tensions grew. In early 1939 the Polish government decided to act against local Ukrainian militants in the region. One day, suspects were rounded up at two o'clock in the morning, taken from their homes, and summarily executed. Such extra-judicial murders only increased tensions between the two peoples.

During the same period Soviet and German propagandists continued to stir mistrust amongst the various ethnic groups in Poland. The Soviets railed against Polish oppressors and greedy landowners who were allegedly exploiting the local Ukrainian population. Meanwhile Nazi spies and local collaborators spread the poison of antisemitism, blaming Jews for every difficulty imaginable. Feelings worsened amongst all the ethnic groups and trust broke down. Secret agents for both neighbouring powers were recruited all around Poland but especially in the east where campaigns to turn the local

Ukrainian population decisively against Polish rule continued through the whole of the nineteen thirties.

There was some but not much inter-marriage, partly because of religious rather than nationalist differences, though the two were deeply inter-connected. Through the 1930s divisions deepened as much of Europe became increasingly nationalistic and extremist. Jan started to become aware of this as a young teenager when going to local Ukrainian villages even though Wladylsaw's reconciliations between Poles and Ukrainians were considerable.

Raising a family

Jan Stepek was the first born in the settlement, on 13 September 1922, arriving two weeks prematurely and therefore one day before his lifelong friend Wladek Wasko. In the first two years of the settlement, 1922 and 1923, most of the couples had their first child so there were lots of children of the same age. As a result of the similar age groups and the newly married status of the couples, a peculiar feature arose in the settlement. There were no older people, no grandparents, and all of the children were of a similar age range. The normal spread of ages from the elderly to newborns was not present in Maczkowce.

Jan remembered little about his earliest years but recalled some of his mother and father's quarrels. Janina once threw eggs at Wladyslaw during an argument. They both seemed to be quick tempered. The young couple, one a political activist, the other a lady brought up to be waited on hand and foot, had to cope with building their home, nurturing the community, bringing up very young children, and working the land.

Jan was the only one of the Stepek children to meet his father's two sisters Helena and Aleksandra in that period, when they came to Maczkowce in the early years of the settlement. There was still friction between the sisters and Janina. They showed off their knowledge of farming and Janina would react by sarcastically suggesting to Wladyslaw that he should have married a local girl who knew something about being a farmer's wife. The aunts never visited Maczkowce again, nor did Wladyslaw bring the children to spend time with the aunts in Haczow. Sadly there were plans to take Danka there for the first time in 1939 but the onset of war prevented the trip from happening.

Jan's two sisters Zofia, known as Zosia, and Maria Danuta, called Danka, were born respectively on 31 January 1925 and 1 July 1927. This completed the Stepek family in Maczkowce.

One of Jan's earliest memories was of travelling on a train to the north of Poland. His impression was that times were bad and there was not enough food in the family home. Janina took Zosia and Jan to stay at the home where two of her sisters lived. Jan was only three or four, so the year would have been 1926 as Danka was not yet born. He remembers being sick on the train and misbehaving at his aunts' house including urinating on the carpet. He tried to persuade his cousin to do the same, but he wouldn't. As one would expect both ended up being severely told off.

Janina's parents visited the family at Maczkowce every summer and stayed for a few weeks. They were very critical of Wladyslaw, particularly of what they perceived to be his failings in the business of farming but were kind to the children. Danka remembers when she was about three her grandfather Jozef hid sweets on top of the grandfather clock for the two girls to find, but Jan used to climb up first and steal them. They remember their grandmother, Joanna, as a very proper lady, sweet and cuddly. Both grandparents died when the children were still young, Jozef in 1930 and Joanna in 1935 when they were in their seventies.

Danka recalls that one of her maternal aunts once visited with the grandparents. She was mentally handicapped and lived with her parents in Nieszawa where they still had some properties. She also remembered that her grandfather seemed very tall and his wife very short. He had a moustache and looked like a gentleman farmer, quite forbidding, and seemed a very practical man. Such was a very young girl's memories of her grandparents.

Jan had some very clear memories of his childhood in general.

"During the summer we were hardly ever in the house as the weather was very warm and pleasant. There was a huge tree and we cooked and had picnics under it. We used to fill a big barrel with water and test its temperature until it was around twenty degrees and then we would have great fun jumping in it. There was no river nearby but the valleys had hollows, possibly ancient lakes. These filled up with rain and snow in early spring and remained until the end of May. We played in these until the water became stagnant then the smell would put us off swimming in them.

In 1929 when I was six years old I started school in the neighbouring village as we didn't have our own school then. The head teacher used to walk me to the school. My mother had brought her to the village to ensure there was local education available. As I grew older I'd walk to school with the other children and we had some good fights on the way, sometimes with other kids from our village and sometimes with Ukrainian or Czech children from neighbouring villages. Quite often, as the eldest child in my village I was in charge and got a good beating from the neighbouring kids which I didn't like. The school itself had been a local police station when it was under Russian occupation, and like the village itself, was poor and rough.

After school in the summer we had hours of continuous play in the fields until it was dark. Then I'd be very frightened walking home along the valleys because of folk tales and fairy stories we'd been told of headless bodies and ghosts. I'd run home as fast as I could without ever looking back in case something grabbed me.

There were regular visits to the school from the local Ukrainian priest, maybe weekly. A protestant minister came frequently too, but we never learned anything of Judaism or received a visit from a rabbi. There were local Ukrainians and Czechs at the school. All the children naturally picked up Ukrainian while at school, not because it was taught but because it was spoken so widely in and around the school.

In the winter I would pour water on the ground to make a skating rink and all the children in the area found this great fun. One year I learned to ski and thereafter I loved to ski to school on home-made skis. In February, rivers would form from the melted snow then freeze and I would skate for what seemed like miles and miles until the stars and the moon came out in the clear frozen sky. I would eventually arrive home shivering with cold and totally tired out; I wanted nothing to eat but instead would go straight to bed without undressing and immediately fall asleep."

After completing primary school in 1933 Jan moved to a state-run secondary school in the city of Luck for one year before moving to another school in Polonka for three years. State schools had a better reputation than privately run ones and were not easy to get into. There were often fights after school between local kids from different villages, often between Ukrainians and Poles, though these were never too serious or violent. Poles were a minority in the region but most teachers were Polish so there was ongoing tension as the Poles ruled the country and tried to maintain control over the unhappy, aggrieved Ukrainian majority in the east of the country.

Although Wladyslaw and Janina were well educated they put no direct pressure on their children to achieve academically. The interests and achievements seemed to stem from the children themselves. They were intellectually curious, unsurprising given the active and dynamic nature of both their parents and the daily interaction with nature on the farm.

In 1935 Wladyslaw organised the construction of a more local school on spare land within Maczkowce, and this opened the following year. It became a state school, taking children from primary and secondary age groups. People from neighbouring villages and settlements sent their children there. There were Germans and Czechs at the new school along with Ukrainians and Poles, and, as the Germans and Czechs were protestant the local pastor visited, as did the Orthodox priest for the Ukrainians. Ironically because there was no priest in the immediate vicinity it was the local teacher who had to teach the Catholic religion. To assist in the teaching needs Wladyslaw arranged for a young woman to come from Haczów to join the school as a teacher.

Jan continued to describe his childhood:

"I never had to look after my sisters when I was very young or be forced to play with them as they were too small and couldn't keep up but we all got on well together. We were free to wander as we pleased so we developed a great love of freedom and a sense of adventure. Of course there was no traffic, only the occasional horse and cart. My perception is that I had a good childhood, a very full life, enjoyable, fun and adventurous. In the spring I would climb the thirty-foot cherry trees right to the top then slip and swing from one branch to the next. We also had hazel nut trees that rose to fifteen or twenty feet and we'd climb and swing on these too."

But Zosia remembers Jan somewhat differently.

"Your father was always the top in everything in school. I was a horrible sister and used to tease him about his height because I was tall, and he was small. He was always helping me, especially to get down from the cherry trees we used to climb to eat the cherries. Once I stayed up for hours unable to get down as I didn't want to ask your father for help yet again. He was very helpful, always protecting us, as he would do so in much worse times.

We had fun in the water in spring floating in barrels pretending to sail down to the Black Sea. I remember skating once and the ice was increasingly fresher and faster till suddenly the ice broke and I went up to my neck in the freezing cold water. I managed to get out but by the time I got back home my clothes were stiff and frozen. I was immediately put in a hot bath and then straight to bed."

Danka, two years' younger than Zosia, had her own childhood memories:

"I never obeyed. I just wouldn't accept what my mother or father said without having my say. If I wanted to go with my father to the orchards because he was spraying the trees, I'd pretend I was ill just before I had to go to school. Mother would feel sorry for me. A short while later of course I miraculously felt better and would spend all day with my father.

I remember a travelling theatre arrived in the area, perhaps in 1937. Our neighbour Mr Wasko got tickets for all of us to go along but my father said I was not to attend, as apparently the show wasn't suitable for younger children. So later on the day of the show I sneaked out of the house, walked on my own to where the theatre was set up, crept in unnoticed by anyone, and went right to the front row. I was really enjoying the show but after a while Jan came up to me.

`You're not supposed to be here` he whispered angrily. `Mum and Dad told me to find you and get you back home.` He had to drag me out of there, with everyone looking at us and laughing at the sight. He had to pull me all the way home. I was furious with him for siding with my parents and he was annoyed at me for wasting his time.

It was the same with food. I was always up to no good. One time I wanted salted herrings, so mother sent our farm labourer to try and find some at a local market or town. He managed to get some but before he came back I had changed my mind.

My sister Zosia on the other hand was always obedient. She never said no and was always for telling the truth until it made me sick. She could knit, she could sew, she could do crochet, and she even went on a cooking course. She could dance too. She was good at everything. Bear in mind she was only fourteen by the time the war broke out, and she could do these things long before then. I eventually learned crochet myself to show myself and my sister that I too could learn at least some skills.

I was good at writing but hated reading. Zosia would sit on my bed and read me stories when I was a young girl which I enjoyed but I thought reading stories myself was a waste of time. I was an outside girl, a real tomboy. The soil on our farm had wonderful red clay and I loved it. It was like an endless toy that nature had given us. We could make so many things out of clay. The Waskos and lots of other children would come round and we'd play at making dolls, carts, animal figures, anything we could imagine with this lovely dirty stuff. Zosia wouldn't touch it; she didn't like getting dirty. I think she was more like a Ciupka, a born lady, a genteel member of the lesser nobility.

But I did look through certain books we had at home. We had two volumes on medicine and health. I would sit and look through these, especially the sections on mushrooms and toadstools. They fascinated me especially as so many varieties grew on our land and in the forests nearby. I learned which ones to pick for food and which were poisonous. My investigations lasted until I picked a new type of mushroom which wasn't in the book so I asked my mother what it was.

She was horrified to learn that I had been going out looking for all the different types and eating the ones I had learned were safe. After that those books disappeared.

It was the same with wheat. Our cook at home used to tell me tales of how her family had to resort to eating different wheats during the First World War when everyone was in danger of starving. I learned from her through my childhood years which wheats were edible and which could not be digested by humans.

For me at that young age I felt Jan and I were like twins although he was five years older than me. I don't know if I was picking up everything about play, nature, and practical ways of doing things from him but if there was a local stream or an area of mud we were always together, he taking care of me while I indulged myself. We'd go climbing trees and he'd pull me up to the higher ones, then one would break and all of a sudden we'd both fall through the lighter branches to the ground. He really looked after me. Mother knew nothing would happen with me if he was there. I used to go checking on the cows and he would come with me. All of this was a massive subconscious learning process under his guidance and care. I was becoming a real farmer girl."

In 1932 the two girls went with their mother for a four to six month stay at the home of Janina's sister Maria and her family in Suwalki, a Polish town of almost 70,000 people near the present-day Lithuanian border. This was the same family that Jan and Zosia had gone to with their mother some six years previously when there was not enough food at home for the family. Janina had been suffering problems with her womb and had to be operated on at a specialist hospital in the north and then allowed to recuperate. She was only twenty-four when she gave birth to Danka, the youngest of her three children. It was unusual for Polish families to have so few children so it is likely that she had had a major condition for some time which prevented her from having any more children. She was thirty by the time of the operation.

Whilst the girls were away from home Jan was working in anticipation of their return. Danka remembers it well.

"I was five so he was only ten yet he cut and shaped wood from branches he had chopped down or broken and from these he made lots of toys. When I came back he showed me one. It was a toy wooden cart. Father went into town and bought me a doll of the right size and we put it inside the cart so I could pull it around and take my dolly for a ride. Jan was so good at practical things, he could do anything.

I started school that year. During the winter, school hours were reduced to a half day lasting from eight o'clock till noon. Then we'd go home for lunch. All the kids used to come to our farm because we had slight hills so they all brought sledges and we'd play in the snow without interruption or adult supervision until supper time. Finally and reluctantly they'd all make their way home in the darkness very tired and they'd go straight to bed.

In the summer we'd play hide and seek in one of the fields. A type of sweet corn grew there which was used as feed for the horses. They grew so tall that no one could see you. Just as in winter all the local children would come. Their parents were from nearby villages, and were friends of our parents. Everyone was treated like family, and there seemed to be no major disputes between the families. It was an unwritten rule that the duty of every adult was to look after the welfare of all the kids when in your fields or home. This didn't need to be accounted for or measured. It was simply the embedded values of the community at large.

We used to hide and climb amongst the trees as well. They grew tall along the main road. Fruits that grew wild or were cultivated as part of people's farms were for everybody. Somehow your own fruit never tasted as good as somebody else's so we just took whatever we wanted. None of the adults complained; it was just accepted that the children could eat as much of anyone's fruit as they liked.

But there was much more to our play than just fun. We were learning so much through our activities and we got to know nature in a deep way. Moreover we were picking up life lessons from the way our parents and the other adults managed and tolerated our play.

Sometimes the adults and government officials would use our enthusiasm and energy for official purposes. We used to go into the nearby forest to look for wild strawberries. At this time in our region people were planting trees as part of a wider government vision of economic development for the country as a whole. We were given one day off school every August and charged with picking up as many seeds as we could of all the different trees that grew in the forest. These would then be sent to Lodz. The official in charge said girls you can pick as many strawberries as you want but remember to pick up the seeds so we can grow little trees. We enjoyed doing these things for the adults; it seemed like fun, as if it was a game. In summertime the forest was absolutely full of blueberries, and a type of strawberry that was white when ripe. We loved all those berries."

Jan also spoke on this theme.

"All three of us were well educated at home but Zosia was the studious one, always top in class, in some ways quiet, but still active. It's hard not be active growing up on a farm.

Zosia was tall for a girl of her age whilst I was small. She was taller than me by the time she was twelve and I fourteen and used to tease me when people would ask who was older. 'I'm the younger one but I'm taller than him' she would say and I would be so annoyed."

When I spoke with Zosia she had one very visual recollection.

"I remember walking with my mother and father through our fields, watching the things grow. They talked about the corn and other crops. I remember all the buildings, all the positions of the farm. The top was enclosed by a pasture. I still remember the names of the cows, the horses, the pigs and chicks and geese, and of course our neighbours."

At harvest time all the children helped, moving from one farm to the next as each harvest was brought in one after the other, like one big extended family comprising the whole settlement. There would be big bonfires set up in the fields after harvest at which potatoes straight from the soil would be baked and smothered in homemade butter. Sour milk and bread were brought by the children from the nearest home to all the farmers and their farmhands working in the fields. When the girls had had enough of the work they would go to the area where the soil was clay and make pretend cakes from it.

Jan knew quite a lot about politics, and when he first started school his teacher was political and very pro-Polish. Jan used to hear his father discussing political issues at home. But it was not always a straightforward case of everyone in public positions being aligned with the ruling regime. Danka said that she learned later in her life that one of her teachers had been secretly working for the Germans. So politics and the education of the young in Maczkowce were often not so innocent.

Wladyslaw was always in the fields or else engaging in politics so Jan didn't remember much of him from his early years except his occasional rows with Janina. But when he was in his teens Jan would go with Wladyslaw in the evenings and listen to his stories about war and politics. They would hold gatherings in the old manor house until this was demolished to make way for the new school.

When Jan finished primary school at the age of eleven in the summer of 1934, his parents decided that a general education was not what was best for him. By this time Jan had already decided he wanted to go to agricultural college, but this couldn't happen until he was at least fifteen. The best secondary school in the region had to be paid for and the family didn't have much money, so Jan went instead to the local secondary school in a Ukrainian village.

Jan was hands on and practical, unlike his father who was cerebral and intellectual by nature. He immediately got into trouble with the local Ukrainian boys. This led to some serious fights, and hardened Jan's views. He outright refused to learn Ukrainian as a language because he felt he already knew it enough to converse with local Ukrainians. But it was also a rebellious and political stance. He said this is Poland and nobody's going to force me to learn Ukrainian in a Polish high school when there was no Polish language studies for those who didn't speak it as a first language. He told his father and Wladyslaw complained to the local government officials, then took Jan out of school. The teacher who insisted on Ukrainian studies lost his job and a Polish teacher took his place. Such were the competing nationalist biases of the times.

Wladyslaw and Janina decided to send Jan to a boarding school for two years in Luck, about an hour's ride away by cart. Jan didn't much like being away from his family but it wasn't a great hardship and he felt he learned a lot during those two years. He did make good friends at the school but at heart he was a quiet teenage boy at this age – between thirteen and fifteen - and most of the others at boarding school were older.

One day in 1936 there was a knock at the door of the farmhouse. This was not unusual as local people often came for advice or pharmacy prescriptions from Wladyslaw. There followed the tale you read at the beginning of this book. Here I'll recount it in more details.

Eight year old Danka opened the door to find a complete stranger before her. That was very rare.

"Hello. Is this the home of Wladyslaw Stepek?"

When Danka said yes, he asked

"Can I speak with him please?"

Danka asked him his name and the man said,

"Tell him my name is Wladyslaw Stepek."

Danka was shocked and ran off to the field where her father was working.

"There's a man with your name at the front door!"

Wladyslaw slowly limped back to the farmhouse.

"Come in, I hear we have something in common. My name is Wladyslaw Stepek too."

The man replied "I know. I am the man who was imprisoned with you in 1915 in Barmuta. I was given your name and your sentence of fifteen years in Siberia for which I was spared the gallows. I was released last year and returned to Poland. Since then I have been trying to find you to say thank you for saving my life."

I think the story bears repeating as it brings together so many of the facets of the lives the Stepeks experienced in those tumultuous years in the thirty of so years that started with the beginning of the First World War and ended just after the defeat of Germany in 1945 in the Second World War. Heroism, bad luck, good luck, political upheaval, attempts to live a normal family life in abnormal times. All of these features of life in those times are captured in that short anecdote.

Being highly educated themselves Jan's parents hoped Jan would change his mind about agricultural college and instead go to university. But eventually they saw things Jan's way. As Jan was to inherit at least one of the farms, they reasoned, he should learn how to manage it properly. But Jan was not the only one keen to learn about the latest farming methods. Janina kept books to report the results of new ways of growing crops, and officials from the Ministry of Agriculture collated reports on how many kilograms per hectare were produced under different methods the family used. Fertiliser practically doubled the yield compared to horse and cow manure. These were some of the earliest records of experimental farming done in Poland.

Jan started agricultural college in the autumn of 1938. He learned about the latest farm machinery and persuaded his father to buy them. But Wladyslaw never learned how to use them well enough. Jan was a very quick learner at such practical matters and soon he was teaching the local farmhands how to work the machines. He was steadily looking after more and more of the running of the farm during each of his holiday periods from college. The farmhands and servants in the house started to learn to accept Jan's instructions as orders.

Danka observed the change in Jan as he grew in confidence and stature within the farm and the family household. In some ways she knew she was losing something special.

"He was my best friend, then he started to grow up. I wanted a little brother but that wasn't to be."

For many years Jan's best friend was Wladek Wasko though they were not particularly close. The other main friend from Maczkowce in those years was Bronek Wawrzkowicz but Jan had fights with him too as well as being friends. Wladek went to the local secondary school – he came from a Ukrainian family background – and Bronek went to college in Lwow. The eldest children of Maczkowce were slowly growing into adulthood but they missed each other's companionship when they were sent to separate schools.

At the end of 1937 Wladyslaw received news that he had been recommended to be awarded the Cross and Medal of Independence, one of Poland's highest military honours, given to those who played a significant part in winning Poland's independence in 1918. But the application was not successful, and the family thought this was because of Wladyslaw's ongoing political activities.

Wladyslaw was increasingly opposed to the military regime that was leading Poland in an increasingly authoritarian, nationalistic and antisemitic direction. His political activities and talks in the region brought him to the attention of the military regime for all the wrong reasons. They particularly opposed his work to try to reconcile all the minority groups in the area, particularly the Jews and Ukrainians, with their Polish fellow citizens. Wladyslaw's work in helping local Ukrainians and Jews with their tax or land issues, and his public rhetoric in favour of equal treatment for all people living in Poland meant he clashed with the nationalistic ideology of the military government.

He was secretly informed by old military friends now in high places that his activities were being discussed at the highest level with a view to arresting him and placing him in the notorious political prison camp, formally known as the Place of Isolation at Bereza Kartuska. This place, as close to a concentration camp that Poland had, was located near Brest in present-day Belarus. It was first used on 12th July 1934 - in a former Russian barracks and prison - and was set up by the Polish President Ignacy Moscicki to inter people who threatened Poland's public security, peace or order. People could be imprisoned there for three months without trial or right of appeal, a period which could be extended by another three months, again without legal process.

In the main those who were incarcerated at Bereza Kartuska were political opponents of the ruling Sanacja regime but some were common criminals. Some sixteen thousand individuals were imprisoned at the centre in its five years of operation, including members of various Ukrainian, communist and peasant parties. Conditions were harsh, including beatings and other forms of torture, prolonged naked exposure to the snow and personal humiliations. Consequently many inmates were released in poor or broken physical and mental state.

The numbers in the prison at any given time was initially around two hundred to five hundred but this soared in 1938 to around seven thousand, with Ukrainians accounting for more than half the total. It is probably during this wave of arrests against Ukrainian terrorism in the east and its political agitation that Wladyslaw found himself being gathered by the same undiscriminating net.

Fortunately for Wladyslaw his friends in high places ensured that the arrest warrant for Wladyslaw's incarceration in Bereza Kartuska was quietly rescinded. As with his earlier sentence by the Russians to go to Siberia in 1915 Wladyslaw had a life-saving escape. In his state of ill-health it is doubtful he would have survived the political detention centre.

The incident serves to illustrate just how tense, fraught and unpleasant the political culture had become in Poland in the late 1930s. The military regime was harsh, though it has to be said not as brutal as some other autocratic regimes in Europe at the time. There was a weakened, but still functioning, parliament who tried their best to limit the most extreme measures of the government. There were constant attempts at subversion from Nazi propagandists, Stalinists, Ukrainian military organisations, and those political opponents who were still free to voice their opinions. This made it hard for Poland to function as anything resembling an open and free society. When one considers the controversial political decisions made in the United Kingdom at the height of The Troubles in Northern Ireland, with internment without trial and the Bloody Sunday massacres of civil rights protestors by British army troops, one can understand the fears and motivations behind the Sanacja regime's most oppressive decisions, even as we can judge and condemn them. It is hard to imagine the pressures on the Polish government in 1938, with Nazi and Soviet psychological pressure on Poland's two borders, and a long-running military-terrorist campaign for independence being run by Ukrainian militia. This was the increasingly fractious atmosphere that the Stepek family lived in through 1938.

Developing The Farm

The farm that was granted to Wladyslaw in 1921 comprised sixteen hectares of land, which is around forty acres, a mid-sized farm for Poland at that time. The initial staple crops on the Stepeks' farm were wheat, oats, rye, barley and potatoes. Over the following years Wladyslaw also planted and matured an orchard which won third prize in a regional competition in the 1930s. He loved working on his orchard and grew skilled in nurturing fruit trees, especially apple which became an area of expertise for him. Other trees included pears, plums, apricots, cherries and peaches. In all, there were more than a hundred trees in the orchard which was fully maturing when war broke out in 1939.

The farm had a windbreak of fir trees running in an east-west direction to protect the young orchard saplings in their early years from the northerly winds. Parallel to the firs was another line of trees. These were walnuts and hazels, which always produced a bumper crop at harvest time.

They grew soft fruit too: strawberries, raspberries, gooseberries, blueberries and blackcurrants. Janina made jam from all these fruits. An extensive vegetable garden grew a variety of crops, including carrots, cabbage, onions and garlic. Turnips were also grown, though not for human consumption; they were for the cattle. In the two years before the war broke out they started growing cauliflowers and

Danka really loved this vegetable, which was new and unusual for her.

The family also kept bees for honey, and Wladyslaw nearly died when one year he reacted badly to a sting.

In addition raising pigs and chickens for meat, the family was self-sufficient in most foods. Beyond food Janina grew flowers around the house which she tended carefully.

As the farm grew and developed over the years the family needed to employ help rather than depend on their neighbours. All the farms were developing so families could no longer spare the time to help each other as much as in the early days. The Stepeks hired three full time farmhands and employed a further four to six seasonal workers from a neighbouring region, Polatia, at harvest time. These people were paid in kind with fruit, vegetables, nuts and grain.

One of the farmhands, Jozef, became a good friend of the three children. From a German family, he had been in the army with Wladyslaw after the First World War but was younger than him. He was treated as one of the family and was completely trusted by everyone. He had unusual physical characteristics: six fingers and six toes on each hand and foot. These features didn't bother him at all, nor did it seem to concern anyone in the locality.

Four or five employees in total lived with the family in the house. One was a cook whom Danka called Babcia, or grandmother, as she became very close to the children. Another was a blacksmith.

The farm was thus developing as a business with staff but the family was not middle-class by today's standards. They made very little money. On the other hand they were far from subsistence level farmers, and culturally they were innovators, educators and intellectually-minded.

Wladyslaw and Janina experimented in farming methods and produce over the years. They bought cows from Holland, but these proved to be too big and heavy in the soft soil of Ukraine. They did however produce an enormous amount of milk. They sold these cows and bought instead local Polish red-brown coloured cows. These had smaller bodies and legs and adapted better to the conditions.

Danka loved the cows, but she loved their milk even more. She would run to the byre with a glass when the two farm-labouring girls were milking the cows. Danka was deemed too young to be allowed to milk the cows herself in case she was kicked. She always took milk from one particular cow which, in Danka's view produced especially sweet milk.

The cows lived on semi-dried grasses in the spring. They were not docile or easy to control like cows nowadays in Scotland. Once, when Jan was fourteen he tried to cajole a cow out of the corn field but the cow refused to move. As Jan shouted at it and became more vociferous the cow decided it had had enough and it was Jan who was chased from the field. Apart from the fields where crops grew the cows had free reign for grazing, from the hillock where the farmhouse stood to the lower slopes of the second hill and beyond, out of site of the farm buildings.

The family had four horses, including a brown one which was Danka's favourite. Alongside the pigs and chickens, Wladyslaw and Janina introduced ducks so there was a sizeable range of livestock on what was a very small farm. The four horses were used for ploughing and for pulling the family cart. The family had a driver for the four-wheel cart which they used to go to the biggest local church, twelve kilometres away in Niescwicz. This was where the three children were baptised. But the family didn't go to church every Sunday; being a rural area the local priest understood that farm work came first, especially at harvest time. In many regards this was the opposite of the biblical view to keep the Sabbath holy.

As the farm developed Janina analysed the financial return on investment of different aspects of the farm. She worked out that pigs created more value than anything else the family were doing so they increasingly focussed their efforts in this area. However after a few successful years the pigs were struck by disease which killed every one of them. In those days there were no vaccinations for animals. A government vet came to inspect the farm and ordered them not to rear pigs for the next seven years so that the disease could be eradicated from the area so the family had to return to other forms of farming.

Janina and Wladyslaw reviewed the options and decided to rear geese. Not only would these produce eggs and meat, but their feathers could be used at home and for sale as filling for duvets and pillows. As a result the whole family had wonderful plump, warm duvets, and things picked up again as a farming business. But as with the pigs, another disease came along and wiped out all the goslings. Seven decades later Danka reflected on this at her daughter's home on another farm in Scotland.

"You may like farming, you may love to rear and take care of animals and that's all well and good. But those things are pleasures and hobbies. Farming at that intimate level is not business, you simply don't make enough money from that way of living and working."

The young farmhand Jozef, or Jozek as the family knew him, married and left the family farmhouse to work for his father-in-law who was a blacksmith. He built a little house near the crossroads not far from the Stepek farm. The young couple had a child and bought a goat and two little kid goats as part of their effort to develop their own farm. Danka used to visit the couple frequently and begged her father to buy the two kids from Jozef. Wladyslaw eventually relented and bought them. They immediately caused havoc, stripping the bark from all the trees in his prized orchard. Eventually however the goats learned and became an important part of the family.

Not all animals were of benefit to the family. For pest control, and as pets, the family kept two cats and two dogs. Mice and rats sometimes plagued the farm, and even the cats couldn't keep up. One day in a fit of frustration Wladyslaw spent all day killing rats at the end of which he counted over two hundred dead. Rabbits were also a nuisance, trying to eat the crops, but foxes were worse. They kept trying to break into the chicken coop. The dogs' job was to chase away the rabbits and foxes. In addition the family had scarecrows to keep the birds away from the seeds and fruit. Crows were the worst culprits in this respect.

Wladyslaw kept homing pigeons for fun, and Jan used to slyly sell them to school friends knowing they would return to his home. Jan's view of farm animals was completely pragmatic. He had no sentimental view of them at all. This was in contrast to Danka who had her horse and a favourite cow, and Zosia, who, seventy years after she last saw the farm could remember the name of each cow. Jan remembered farming as a constant slog for little return, and the animals simply useful produce for the family.

Jan did remember that it wasn't only people who had an unromantic view of other animals. One day he was clearing the stables and byre and noticed one of the pigs snuggling up to the nearest horse for warmth. The horse edged away. The pig got up and snuggled in once more, at which point the horse bent over, grabbed the pig by the neck with its teeth and threw the poor squealing animal as far from it as it could manage. The pig learned its lesson and lay in the cold hay nursing its wounds and, if pigs have pride, nursed that too.

The farm animals were often more than a match for the family members. Jan remembers a time in 1936 or 1937 being bitten on the arm by a horse as he tried to pull it back into the stable.

Wladyslaw started to experiment with using industrial fertiliser as opposed to horse and cow manure. This was an innovation encouraged by the central government in Poland. Janina would keep the books and records of which farming techniques worked and which failed. Unlike most farmers they didn't use the same crops or grains each year but tried different types to see how yields varied. The Polish government was actively involved in these practical experiments and all records were sent to them. Wladyslaw taught his neighbours and other local farmers the theory of letting land lie fallow. As a chemist he understood about the science of nature and how different elements contributed to the greater success of growing crops.

Sometimes however these experiments went dangerously wrong as experiments do. Cropping was generally very reliable but Wladyslaw felt that the soil was too good to use for oats and other cheap crops. He was in essence a pioneer, and in any business of course this does not always guarantee success. One year, around 1930 he decided to plant only a particular type of wheat which matured several weeks after the other crops his neighbours were growing. It proved to be an excellent crop through the spring and early summer, and the experiment looked to be a great success. The market price per kilogramme was much higher than his usual crop so things were looking very promising.

After everyone else's crops had been harvested and only the Stepek's new super wheat remained in their fields a severe hailstorm came and flattened the wheat. They lost it all. This meant the family had to kill all of their pigs as they had no wheat with which to feed them. This was a disaster for them as a family. They would have starved had Janina and the girls not travelled to spend the winter months at Janina's sister's home leaving Jan and Wladyslaw to survive the winter alone. It was primarily bad luck but Wladyslaw had put all his eggs in one basket and learned a harsh lesson. Jan took these lessons with him in his later life; don't be a pioneer, he would say, and remember to spread your risks.

In his year at agricultural college in Bojanowo in 1938-39 Jan was increasingly allowed to influence the running of the farm. Wladyslaw was doing a good job of succession planning, always a difficult and challenging transition in family businesses, especially in farms. As his health declined

Wladyslaw was grooming Jan to take his place, knowing that his son was learning modern ways of farming.

Jan said of his father and his farming methods:

"I got on with my father but I was fairly contemptuous of him. He was hopelessly impractical and with the arrogance of youth I thought I was good at everything to do with farming and business. Of course in those days I didn't take full account that he was in fact an invalid, with a lung removed from the time he had TB during the First World War so he didn't have the physical energy to handle the relentless nature of farm work."

Wladyslaw went to Warsaw from time to time to visit the Agricultural Ministry, bringing his farming statistics for the government and he would explain what was happening. But for all his high standing and analysis he was not a very practical man. Jan remembers one day in 1939 when Wladyslaw could not fix part of the farm's machinery. Jan took it from him, fixed it in a few minutes and gave it back to him, shaking his head. It was like a family scenario in our own times but with mobile phones or other new technology. The better educated group among the younger generation in Poland at that time were becoming more familiar with industrial machines and farming techniques.

Ultimately Wladyslaw was more interested in politics than farming. He developed his ideas for the farm from books on agriculture and tried to implement the ideas he read about. But many of these ideas were experimental and when you pioneer you often fail so the Stepeks found their innovative efforts sometimes let them down.

As he studied agriculture as an academic subject for the first time at college Jan developed his own vision and ideas for growing the farming business. He was thinking of buying a mill and exporting grain to western Europe. In this thinking he was following the expertise of his mother's family, the Ciupkas, and he could rely on their know-how and their many international business contacts to help him bring his vision to fruition. By the summer of 1939 he had a clear vision of his future in Poland.

Last Days as Family, Last Days for Poland

As Christmas neared in December 1938 all was not well in the Stepek household. The children's lives were normal. Jan was about to complete his first term at agricultural college, still boarding at Bojanowo, his imagination fired by ideas for creating new businesses related to farming. Grain exports, mills, maybe even brickworks like his Ciupka uncles and aunts. Zosia was in her second year of high school, beginning to think of a future where education, reading and learning would continue to play a part. And Danka was in her last year of primary school, reluctantly doing what it took to satisfy the teachers but far more interested in real life, learning through play, by exploring nature, and by trying things out to see what happened.

Wladyslaw was suffering, and Janina was worried for him. His health, never good, continued to deteriorate as winter came round, and he was persuaded to visit the doctor. In turn the doctor sent him to the nearest hospital and the diagnosis was not what anyone wanted to hear.

He was told that he had a major ailment. Unless he was operated on he may die within a matter of weeks. Reluctant to commit one way or another Wladyslaw agreed to be kept in hospital under observation up to and past Christmas Day.

The house was therefore a miserable place, with everyone worried and missing Wladyslaw. Janina telegraphed the bad news to Jan and suggested that he should either stay in Bojanowo, or if he wanted family at Christmas, travel to Warsaw and stay with his cousins there.

By the time Christmas Eve arrived Danka was suffering from a fever, most likely symptoms of the flu. Her temperature soared and Janina soothed her from time to time with cool cloths to her forehead and face. This was leading up to the worst Christmas the family had ever had. To make matters worse all the news from Europe was intensely worrying for Poland. Germany had swallowed up Austria and parts of Czechoslovakia. Everyone felt it was only a matter of time before Poland was in a state of war.

As evening came Danka started to moan. Janina came to help her but Danka was mumbling words that were almost inaudible. Finally Janina heard her say

"Janek is at the station. You need to go get him."

Janina said "No, it's OK dear. He's staying in Warsaw remember? Settle down now."

"No he's here. He's at the station and wants a lift home." said Danka.

There was no way of stopping Danka repeating this. She was quite frantic. Then there was a knock on the door. It was a neighbour.

"I passed your son Janek at the train station. Do you want me to head back and give him a lift? I couldn't do it before as there wasn't any space in the cart."

A half hour later the neighbour dropped Jan off at the door. He had decided at the last minute that, even if Christmas was to be sad without their father, he'd still rather be home than at college or with his relatives. This lifted the family's spirits, and they didn't know what to make of Danka's premonition.

An hour later Wladyslaw walked in.

"If I'm going to die I'd rather do it here at home than in some hospital bed." He said. "Anyway it's nearly Christmas so let's celebrate it as family, together, and be grateful for what we have."

And so a few hours later, as Christmas Eve gave way to the 25th December 1938 the Stepek family of Maczkowce brought in Christmas together. They were never to do so again.

Part 3 War

The Outbreak of War

The summer of 1939 brought even more foreboding. Czechoslovakia, Poland's neighbour had now been completely occupied by the Nazis. In turn the British and French recommitted themselves to the defence of Poland should it be attacked. This at one level was reassuring but many of those in Poland remembered the First World War and the carnage it brought, so even though the might of France and Britain might ensure a victory in any war with Germany that would take a long time. There seemed likely to be war at any rate.

In late summer Jan decided not to return to his studies in Bojanowo. He felt sure that war was coming. What was the point of studying when it was likely to be brought to a standstill within months. So the family just did what farming families did every summer. They worked in readiness of harvest time, and with Jan now approaching seventeen, Danka had to rely on her school friends to play with in the fields and climb the nearby trees. Zosia tried to enjoy the beauties of the season but she was a thinker, and with thinking comes worries. What was awaiting them all? What was the fate of Poland to be?

Staying with the family that summer was Janina's sister-in-law, also called Janina, and her daughter Dobrusia, who was Danka's age. They lived in Warsaw with Janina Stepek's brother Waclaw, but they felt it would do the mother and daughter good to experience some countryside at such a tense time.

The moment everyone dreaded came on 1st September 1939 when Germany finally burst the tension that had been building up over Europe that year. Less than a month earlier, to the astonishment of the world Germany signed a non-aggression treaty with the Soviet Union. Unknown to the world a secret protocol had also been agreed between the two states that, on conquering Poland, Germany would annexe the western half, leaving the east to the Soviet Union. Hitler now felt sure he could invade Poland without the risk of a counter-attack by the Soviet Red Army

It took until 17th September for the Soviet armed forces to invade eastern Poland, by which time Poland was nearing defeat. All its remaining forces were engaged in desperate struggle to hold onto whatever areas remained in Polish hands. When the Red Army marched in they were virtually unimpeded and Poland's fate was sealed. Neither France nor Britain had made any serious attempt to attack Germany.

That day, 17th September, the first Soviet troops entered the farmlands in and around Maczkowce, along with NKVD officers. These were the precursors to the KGB and were the Soviet Union's internal security force, a dreaded secret police.

The Stepek family awaited the actions of the invading army with apprehension. They were not to wait long. That evening a Jewish friend of Wladyslaw turned up at the door of their farmhouse.

"I have heard that you are to be arrested and immediately shot. They have a list of potential troublemakers, those who may lead local resistance. You are one of two in the district."

As Wladyslaw considered what options he had, a Ukrainian friend appeared at the door.

"Wladyslaw, they are coming for you within the hour. They will take you out, and they will kill you without a trial, without any formalities. You need to leave, and you need to leave right now. Let me take you across to the German side, to the nearest train station and then you can go where you think you may be safest."

Janina urged him to go, so reluctantly he left his family and set off for the newly imposed German-Russian border in his friend's cart, both of them hiding rifles under the blankets on their laps. He told Janina that he would aim for Haczow.

On the way they passed a village where a young Ukrainian communist recognised Wladyslaw and knew he was one of those targeted for execution. He took out his rifle and prepared to shoot Wladyslaw, but his mother intervened, begging her son not to kill him, so he relented.

They had no further incidents before arriving at the tiny train station where Wladyslaw said his thanks and goodbye to his friend. But on the way home the Ukrainian friend was stopped and arrested for helping Wladyslaw escape.

He was asked to reveal where Wladyslaw was, as the Red Army suspected he would stay in the local area in hiding. The friend stated that Wladyslaw had died, and he had buried him. He showed them one of the many newly-dug graves in the area and said this was where he had buried Wladyslaw. The occupying army couldn't be certain whether he had told the truth or lied, but they told Janina and her children that Wladyslaw was dead, not saying how or when. Over the next weeks the family didn't know whether to believe them or not as they heard nothing about or from Wladyslaw.

The Ukrainian friend was tried by a new people's commission made up of Ukrainian supporters of the Soviet occupiers, and found guilty of aiding the enemy. For this he was sentenced to several years in Siberia. He was released in 1942 and immediately joined the Polish armed forces that were sent to Egypt. Wladek Wasko, one of the eldest children in Maczkowce, was in Egypt two years later and met the man who had helped Wladyslaw – so on his return, Wladek was able to pass the information on to the Stepek family.

The situation in the eastern half of Poland was now extremely complex and dangerous. As there was no ethnic majority population, there was no dominant view on which side to support in the war as it now played out.

The vast majority of ethnic Poles opposed the Soviet invasion. Poles were overwhelmingly Catholic so the atheist and anti-religious doctrines of communism had little support for the faithful. Moreover Russia had been considered an imperial force for over a century by most Poles, and the change from Czarist to Bolshevik leadership did not change most Poles' view that the Russians were to be opposed under any circumstance. However some Poles were members of the illegal communist party in the country. Taking into account sympathisers to that cause perhaps no more than two percent of ethnic Poles were communist, even though a significant minority of ethnic Poles were left-leaning socialists.

Among the Ukrainian people there was a full spectrum of reaction to the invasion, complicated by the desire of many Ukrainians to achieve their own nation state. Many of the extreme nationalists sided with the Soviet invasion reasoning that out of the chaos of war there was an opportunity to win independence. Moreover many of these were the fiercest haters of ethnic Poles, often with little love for Jews or other minorities too.

Others were at the opposite extreme. They had lived in peace with the Poles and Jews for decades, had no ill-will towards any group, and had no wish for anyone to be harmed in the horrors of war. They had all experienced a traumatic war only twenty-one years earlier and didn't want to face it again.

Others sat in the middle. Pro-Ukrainian, and generally with a view that the Polish government had mistreated them, they wanted a better life for themselves and their fellow Ukrainians but not at the expense of wholesale repression of the local Poles.

The position of the Jews in the region was complex and sensitive. Many ethnic Poles, even today, say that a higher percentage of Jews than Poles welcomed the Soviet invaders, that Jews were more likely to be communists than other groups. I have been unable to find any robust evidence for this. Most Jews would have been fearful of Poles and Russians alike. Growing anti-semitic legislation by the Polish government in the late 1930s made them wary of the Poles' attitudes towards them. The history of pogroms against Jews when eastern Poland was under Russian Czarist rule lived still in the collective memory of the Jews of the east of Poland. Being a race with a history of being mistreated, Jews may have felt more sympathy for the vision of communism as a movement that sought to liberate the oppressed from greedy landlords and rulers. But from two facts we do know – one percent of all Poles were known to be communist; Jews comprised almost ten percent of the Polish population – then simple mathematics tell us that at least ninety percent of Jews were not formally communist.

What is certain is that a Ukrainian and a Jewish friend risked their lives to save Wladyslaw Stepek.

It is most important to reiterate that in the heat of this war as in any situation there was no such thing as "the Poles" or "the Ukrainians" or "the Jews". There may be evidence showing that a higher percentage of one minority than others favoured communism, the Soviet invasion, Ukrainian military aggression, or any other political position; but it is always wrong to state that an entire people ever had a single view on any matter.

The Red Army and those Ukrainian militants who formally sided with the Soviets were frustrated that Wladyslaw had eluded their grasp. So between late September 1939 and early January 1940 they terrorised the Stepek family. They took Janina from her home for several days without telling the children why, or where she was.

When she returned her hair had turned grey and she was clearly a broken woman. The children never asked what happened and she never spoke of it, except to say that she had been kept in an open pit dug so deep she could not climb out and was kept there day and night without any shelter or means with which to defend herself from men, animals or the elements. Based on testimony of similar aggression to women elsewhere in the region at the time it is likely that she had been tortured, beaten and raped. Partly this abuse would have been in order to force her to reveal where Wladyslaw was hiding, but also tragically because this is what some human beings do when given positions of power during a war.

Combinations of Ukrainian men and Red Army soldiers would come into the Stepek house at any time of day, trash the furniture and shelves, take away anything they liked the look of, and smashed the religious icons or paintings on the walls. They sometimes put all four family members up against the kitchen wall as they did so.

One time they put a gun to Jan's head.

"Tell us where Stepek is or we'll shoot the boy" they said.

The family never revealed Wladyslaw's whereabouts and the terrorisers never pulled the trigger.

Christmas came and went, as did New Year. They were conducted in an atmosphere of deep fear and worry with nothing to bring any cheer.

But in early January this changed. The Red army intercepted a letter from Wladyslaw to Janina saying that he had made it to Haczow. A Russian soldier informed Janina that her husband was alive in Haczow, an act of great kindness. The soldiers and militants now knew he was not in their territory and that he was not important enough to ask the German authorities to try to find him, so they relented and left the Stepek family alone.

However, though it started with good news, 1940 was to bring an even-greater crisis to the Stepeks.

Deportation 10 February 1940

It was the classic tactic of bewilderment and fear. Wake them up in the dead of night when everyone is sound asleep. A sharp rap of rifle butts on the front door, voices shouting, "Open up!", shouting "Hurry up! Open the door!"

The process had begun earlier in the evening on the 9th of February 1940. The Soviet administrators had called a meeting of each householder in the settlement. Instructions were given of new ways to fell the trees and how they were to be transported. Every family was ordered to get their horse and carts ready that night so that they could be ready to start the new work schedules the following morning at dawn. In the meantime, they were to remain at home.

Similar work projects involving felling trees in the area had been going on in the previous few weeks, so no one was surprised or alarmed by this new set of instructions. Only in retrospect did the Soviet plan become clear.

At two o'clock in the morning of the 10th February 1940 the cleansing of Maczkowce began. In the Stepeks' case it was two Ukrainian militia men who entered their home, with a Soviet Red Army soldier. Brusquely the family were told,

"Dress. Take food for a few days, put it in the cart, and all of you get in. Go where you're told."

The Red Army commander in charge quietly told Janina to take all she could, including protection against the cold. So the family hurriedly packed the little savings they had, salt, bread, meat, a sack of flour, plus warm clothing, duvet covers and blankets.

Everyone who was in Maczkowce that night was removed. No consideration was made for the elderly, the sick, the disabled, or the very young. Nor was there any consideration given for families who had one or more members absent at that time.

Janina, Jan, Zosia and Danka, together with their cousin Dobrusia and her mother, also Janina, drove in their packed cart towards the nearest train station, Dobawa Karczma, as instructed. They knew the situation meant they were being taken somewhere but had no inkling that none of them were ever to return to their home or the region.

They found themselves in a sad procession of carts filled with neighbours and friends for twenty years and more, and for the whole lives of the children and teenagers. It was pitch black and one of the coldest days for years, around minus thirty degrees centigrade.

This was not just a local action. In farms, villages, towns and cities from the far south to the border with Lithuania, the same scene was being enacted. A full-scale deportation of the families of the military settlers of 1921 was taking place. It was to be the first of a four-fold wave of deportations to cleanse the western half of Ukraine of all Poles who were deemed to be potential resisters to the occupying Red army and their local allies. Others to be deported were simply of the landowning classes perceived as oppressors and exploiters of the peasant population in the annexed eastern half of Poland.

The majority of those deported were ethnic Poles, but a significant minority were Jews, Ukrainians, Belarusians, Lithuanians and others from minority groups in the borderlands. This fact confirms the complex reality of the spectrum of social and political views in the region. Many Ukrainians did not welcome the Soviet invasion, nor did they hate the Poles. Similarly, many Jews and other minorities were actively resistant to the invaders and desirous of the continuation of the Polish state. Others however did welcome the Soviets, either because they were themselves communist, or because they were anti-Polish. It is important when exploring history not to make national stereotypes or make simplistic statements about what is always a nuanced and complex reality.

Numbers vary widely as to how many Polish citizens were deported to the Soviet Union in this way. Much depends on who was counted, and for what reason they were removed. The minimum number from Soviet sources at the time, and from modern Russian and Polish research suggests around 300,000 people. By the widest definition a number of one million seven hundred thousand can be reached. However, the actual number is academic: there is a danger in focussing too much on the numbers. One can lose sight of the enormity of the suffering and human tragedy that occurred.

It was at the station, Dobawa Karczma, that the family realised something of the full extent of the cleansing. They saw virtually the entire community of Maczkowce, and others from nearby settlements. In the half light of pre-morning the families were ordered onto cattle trains, adapted crudely for the new human cargo. Two tiers of beds made of wooden planks lined the wagons. On the upper one a person could sit half bent, but on the bottom one you could only lie down. Fifty people were put in each of these carriages. In the centre of the wagon an iron stove had been fixed in place, providing the possibility of heat for warmth or cooking, should coal, wood and food be available. Everyone was dumbstruck at the condition of the wagons. They were still barely awake, numb with the cold, and now they were even more frightened.

When everyone was in the heavy sliding doors were shut with a bang but they were not to move off for more than a day. Finally the train started to move. Many cried. Others, sensing an ominous future, started to sing patriotic songs, or hymns, or silently said prayers.

The days on their journey passed slowly. One day became another, then another and another until most of the weary, freezing travellers lost all sense of time or place. A few people kept diaries. From time to time they looked outside the small metal grill that served to allow air into the otherwise crammed wagon. They were looking for signs, names of stations they passed, to get some idea of where they were heading.

People experienced a bizarre combination of feeling frozen on some parts of the body whilst other parts were sweating from proximity to other people, or to the stove. This was used mostly to heat water, obtained by breaking icicles off the underside of the roof.

There was always a queue for use of the stove. A heavy smell of sweat and damp clothing hung thick all day and night in every nook and cranny of the wagon.

A hole had been cut out of the floor near the wall behind the stove. It was 15cm in diameter and acted as a toilet. In the first few days a family member held up a blanket to enable some privacy for those using the hole. Eventually someone pinned up blankets as a more permanent arrangement. During the coldest days this hole would freeze over whilst no one was using it, then it became a matter of the greatest urgency and desperation to smash the ice and allow the person to do the toilet. The urgency stemmed from the dysentery which many of the passengers suffered.

Some people, generally the oldest and the very young, became more and more sick. One death became two, became several, till people stopped counting. Their bodies would have to stay in the locked wagons until at random, days apart, they were opened. Then the bodies were taken out by the deportees, buried if time allowed, otherwise placed onto the snow in the middle of nowhere.

After an unknown period but looking back it may have been two to four days into the journey, the train came to a stop. The wheels were changed. This meant only one thing, that they had come to a border, most likely at the Soviet Union, because the Soviet train system ran on different sized tracks than the Polish railway. Jan sensed this quickly, and guessed that they were being taken to Siberia, or what the Poles called Siberia, which meant those parts of Russia that were most remote. Many Poles who rose against Russian occupation during the nineteenth century were sent into exile in different parts of Russia. The Poles lumped all these areas into one name, Siberia, which was uttered with dread. History now seemed to be repeating itself, only this time not to nationalist or political rebels, but families comprising the old, women, children and babies.

The train didn't travel smoothly or continuously. It moved excruciatingly slowly. Problems with engines, and a lack of replacement parts caused delays for hours on end, on some occasions, days. The train would be shunted into sidings where snow drifted onto the walls of the wagons threatening to completely cover the train.

Occasionally they would stop at a station, usually with no sign of a name to identify where they were. Here the Poles were allowed out, able to stretch properly in the freezing cold. Those with money could buy a bucket of soup and brick-shaped bread from the local people who always seemed to emerge from nowhere wherever a train stopped.

Nor did the train go in a simple single direction. It changed direction time and again, seemingly without reason. Through these first two weeks they saw a multitude of similar trains with faces peering out of the gridded window. More Poles it seemed. So many Jan imagined that perhaps the entire Polish population of the eastern region had been deported.

Eventually, no matter how carefully they rationed it, the family ran out of food. Worse, there were days on end when they had no access to water. Any water was boiled carefully in order to eradicate organisms that could cause disease. Everyone was in the same position, and as hunger and thirst grew in the bitter cold, people's spirits and health started to break down. This was exacerbated by the growth in the number of lice that seemed to occupy every area of the beds, the floor, the ceiling. Meanwhile outside, as people took turns at the tiny window, the landscape became increasingly bleak; white, treeless, devoid of houses, flat like a frozen ocean.

Having witnessed deaths on the train and grieving for their homes and the seeming peace and security of Poland, all those on board longed for the freezing journey to end.

Arrival

Almost three weeks after they were taken from their homes, the train finally ended its journey and the weary passengers disembarked. They discovered that they were at the northern Russian town of Kotlas, in Archangel Region, the northernmost part of the Soviet Union, which spans the Arctic Circle and reaches towards the North Pole. Kotlas, today a town of 82,000 people, lies at the confluence of two major rivers, the Vychegda and Dvina. It was 1st March 1940, a date registered by the officials in the region as their date of arrival into their jurisdiction.

During the first day and night the train doors were left open so people could use it as a place to rest or sleep but they were now free to come and go as they pleased. After this the deportees were taken as one single group to an old Russian Orthodox monastery on the outskirts of town, and there they stayed for several days.

One day an order went out that the group had to take all their belongings, load any possessions and young children onto sledges, and set off into the snowy surrounds, the adults following the sledges on foot. This order was executed very speedily and some families found themselves separated from each other because a family member had gone down to the river to fetch water, or another person was bartering for some food when the order came through.

All the families which comprised the main farming settlement of Maczkowce had been taken together as far as the monastery outside Kotlas. Now the deportees were selected to go to one of two camps, roughly splitting the Maczkowce population into two equal groups. Jan found out after the war that the other half of the Maczkowce deportees had been sent to a camp that was once notorious as a political labour camp. It had been reserved for people deemed enemies of the state at the height of Stalin's purges only a few years' earlier. Stories of past torture, murder and mass disappearances circulated.

The first night after Kotlas they rested in another orthodox church, this time truly ancient. So many people were crammed into it that they kept each other warm against the deeply biting cold outside, yet the frost was severe and seemed to get colder with the morning.

Off they set again, on foot, slowly trudging after the sledges. For some that's where their journey ended; weakened by the long gruelling journey from Poland people died in the snow. They were placed to the side and simply left behind. Others collapsed, and though still breathing could not be carried or awoken from their exhausted sleep. They too were left, where the wind and the cold would finish them off within hours. No graves, no marking place for their families to return to in order to remember them.

Day followed day until they lost track of what day of the week it was or what date. And then they arrived. A set of wooden barracks stood beside a small settlement on the banks of a massive river which was still mostly frozen over. Here they were told the name of the place that was to be their home for the foreseeable future: Charytonowo.

Charytonowo

They were told it was now 10th March 1940. It had been a full month since they had been forced to leave their homes and Poland. They had travelled fifteen hundred miles by cattle train. Charytonowo is at 61.2 degrees latitude, about 360 miles south of the Arctic Circle, and 47.3 degrees longitude making it almost as far east as Teheran. Alternatively spelt Kharitonovo, the labour camp to which half of the population of Maczkowce were deported lies on the banks of the River Vychegda, a 702 miles long tributary of the Northern Dvina river, about thirty miles north-east of Kotlas. In springtime the Vychegda grows to a mile wide as the winter snows and ice melt.

Winter is unusually long in this region, about two hundred and fifty days from early September to the end of April and is extremely cold with temperatures averaging minus fifteen degrees Fahrenheit (minus twenty-six degrees Celsius) combined with frequent strong winds. Fortunately, the family had taken a lot of clothes with them, as it had already been the coldest recorded winter in Poland's history even before they were transported.

Spring comes late but quickly in this region, in late April or early May, and life blossoms fully into Summer for around three months followed by a very short Autumn. The average summer temperature is about fifty-nine degrees Fahrenheit (fifteen degrees Celsius).

The location was near where the Nobel-Prize winning author and dissident Alexander Solzhenitsyn was held just a few years later. The nearest village to the camp was called Workuta, a few days by boat from Kotlas, except in winter when the river was completely frozen over. The four members of the young Stepek family were now twelve hundred miles from their home as the crow flies and eight hundred miles further north.

It was not only Poles who were sent to Kotlas during this period. It was the transport hub from where peoples of many different regions were sent onwards to a multitude of labour camps that made up a sizeable part of the whole Gulag labour camp system. Russians, Lithuanians, Ukrainians, Finns, and Jews were all transported there. Jan estimated that there must have been around thirty to forty successive waves of deportees brought to the monastery at Kotlas in the time the Stepeks were at the camp, based on the number of people who eventually came to the barracks and surrounding camps.

The settlement didn't look like a prison camp, more like a military compound, with every building made from wood. The camp itself consisted of a series of around thirty to forty communal living quarters and smaller houses. Some small shops existed for basic provisions, though often these had nothing in them for days or weeks. There were separate shops for workers, for teachers, and one for NKVD and other officials. Inside the barracks, where two to three families were allocated to each building, people bathed in large basins, with blankets pinned up for privacy. The boards of the barrack floors were almost white from years of scrubbing with sand and stone; and to keep this arduous task to a minimum everyone removed their shoes – assuming they had any – at the threshold and walked barefoot inside.

On arrival the adults were told 'you'll have no sex and no new babies. You won't have the energy'.

There were more people living locally in small villages up to three or four miles away. The deportees didn't have any connections with them initially but as time went by the Poles and the locals warily started to get to know each another. Jan found out that the local people were themselves descendants of deportees from across the Russian empire during Tsarist times. Clean-living, they had small timber houses that resembled huts. These were intricately held together by wooden pegs without the use of any nails.

The civilian deportees were separated from political prisoners, dissidents, and criminals who, rumour had it, were in a labour camp nearby. Word got out that things were much worse there.

The family were surprised to discover that there were Russian-speaking Poles amongst the local people. They were Soviet citizens, sentenced in the 1930s to live in the area as part of a major repression of the Polish minority in the Soviet

Union at that time. Mostly professionals, doctors, lawyers, scientists, they were scared to talk with the newly arrived Polish deportees. They didn't want to be seen to be causing any trouble. They knew at first-hand the consequences of simply being noticed, and how the hand of fate could crush anyone at any time in Stalin's Soviet Union. This group looked down on the newly deported Poles as ill-educated peasant farmers.

Most locals however were Ukrainian, survivors of hundreds, perhaps thousands who had been deported to clear the then virgin forest area in the early 1930s. A massive, orchestrated famine had led to innumerable deaths in the Ukrainian part of the Soviet Union, and deportation was part of the same genocidal policy. The locals told the story that the Ukrainians had just been dropped off in the forest, given axes and ordered to build barracks. It was they therefore who built the shelters that the Stepeks and other Polish families now lived in. Until they did so they had to sleep on the bare ground. They had been given no rations of food, so they foraged in the woods for berries, mushrooms, anything edible. They made bread with any materials they could find, including strips of birch bark but winter came and not all of the barracks were yet complete, so it was difficult for everyone to survive.

A story was told to the newly arrived Poles of a white hillock some miles away from the camp, which rose surreally from the otherwise flat bog-like terrain. Apparently in the early 1930s over a thousand Ukrainian exiles were working in that area in the winter, building barracks. As the early winter darkness grew the guards forced the workers to stay overnight on the hillside. This made it easier for the guards to keep an eye on the workers while they, the guards, warmed themselves from the bitter cold wind by fires lit around the base of the hill.

The following morning the guards went to get the men back to work but there was no movement from the workers. Every single one had frozen to death. Because of the scale of the ice and snow around them, the bodies were just left and as winter continued the bodies became covered in snow and forgotten about. It was only with the sudden onset of spring that the snow started to melt. When it did the hillock remained white with the bleached skeletons of the dead.

A few months after they arrived in Charytonowo they heard that several Finns had been brought in nearby, but this was never corroborated. The place was abuzz with rumours, of supposed transports of dissidents and news about the war. There were stories of local prisons and camps, and cells for foreigners. In a country in which misinformation and disinformation was a daily political and social tool it was impossible to know what was true, rumour, gossip, or a lie.

The locals had a very fatalistic view of their situation, something they readily shared with the new arrivals. "Here you've come and here you'll stay" they told Jan as he got to know them, but Jan always answered that one day they would leave this place. It seemed an implausible optimism.

The administration and command of the camp was not military, but civilian, employees of the NKVD. These people were in effect sentenced just as much as the Poles, as none had a choice in where they were posted and lived almost as harsh and poor a life as the deportees.

Once all the families had been given places to live, jobs were allocated. The administrators asked people what professions or skills they had. The main work was clear from the start; to cut down trees, manage their movement to the river, and float them in huge numbers downstream to the confluence of the Vychegda and the mighty Dvina, from where the logs would be taken up towards the city of Archangel.

However, related to this work there was a huge demand for joiners and carpenters to use smaller logs to make domestic goods such as chairs, stools and tables, and for maintaining and repairing the barracks and other buildings.

Zosia was allocated work at the riverside, numbering the felled logs as they were stacked up. Jan too was given work in the forest, trimming felled trees, but this gave him severe stomach pains due to the combination of the physical effort of lifting timber and the freezing temperatures. Jan made up a story that he had trained in joinery before the war, so the commandant offered him alternative work in a workshop where stools and chairs were being made. This afforded Jan the luxury of collecting spare timber for fire to keep the labourers warm in the workshop. Such a privilege was not available to those like Zosia who had to work outside.

Jan had in fact learned a little carpentry at high school and had some knowledge of trees both from growing up on a farm with forests nearby, and from his more recent studies at agricultural college. More importantly he was immediately aware of the dangers of being allocated to work felling the trees. If the remorseless winter cold didn't kill you, the trees falling in all directions probably would.

He was taken to a workshop, given a pile of wood and access to a nearby machine, and told to make stools based on one given to them as an example of the finished result. Having cut their wood to approximately the right dimensions each carpenter then had to join a queue to use the machine to more accurately shape the wooden parts of the stool. This was to be done for each part of every stool each person was making so it was a hugely inefficient and tedious process. Moreover, the workers were given targets. If they failed to reach them their food rations were cut, but if they exceeded targets, they might be given a few extra roubles with which to buy something basic like bread or eggs at one of the shops, or to buy something a little different from one of the local people.

Jan made his first stool. Having waited in turn to use the machine he tried his best to copy the template. It was a complete failure so he quickly burned it so no one would see that he was not a competent carpenter. He decided he had to rethink his approach altogether. In order to become competent at the tasks in hand, when it was his turn at the machine, he didn't just shape three stool legs and one seat to make a single stool but, much to his fellow carpenters' annoyance and derision, he made eighty stool legs in one period at the machine. This gave him the opportunity to learn how to do the task of honing a stool leg to perfection, and how to do it quickly and effectively.

However it also meant that he had no finished stools that day, only a large number of legs. The supervisors criticised him and sent him away with only half his food rations, which he had to share with his family. So it went on day after day. Jan worked on the machine making either only legs or only seats for the stools, but still didn't put them together to make the finished article. Only when he had enough parts, and enough time to put them all together did he leave off the machine work and start to make stools with all the parts. As with the tooling jobs, because he could now focus solely on putting the parts together, he found with each stool he could do it better and more quickly.

A week or so later, having gone hungry because of lack of food as a punishment for not producing enough stools, Jan finally triumphed. He had completed as many as several of his fellow detainees put together. He received the top pay and bonuses, and extra food. At this early stage of their detention Jan was the only family member working so what he earned, in food and money, had to be enough for four people.

Jan's success continued but there was a downside. The work became an endless treadmill. Starting before dawn he returned exhausted to the barracks well after dark, completing a daily average of around twelve hours work.

After two months spring made its hugely welcome arrival. Zosia was made to work at the riverside, numbering the felled logs as they were stacked up. The days grew longer each day and work eventually continued until the late spring daylight reluctantly gave way to a few hours of darkness. Zosia had to work until the supervisors allowed her to stop. Usually this was relatively reasonable but at times the hours of working seemed to last forever. Exhausted, Zosia feared that she might fall asleep and be swept into the river by the logs being toppled or rolled down the slopes towards the riverbank.

In some areas the trees were dragged two kilometres from where they were cut down. Positioned above the river, they were first piled one on top of another, held in place by massive wooden wedges which had ropes attached to them. This was where Zosia counted and numbered each trunk.

Then on the instructions of the supervisor, men pulled away the retaining supports and the mass of trunks toppled down into the river to be taken downstream by the current.

Theoretically the Poles were free and they were paid a little depending on their work rate. So, in one sense they were free to go, but they had no resources and of course they could never survive the cold. Some people did try, only to freeze in the cold wasteland. They were brought back, bodies frozen stiff. The lesson was quickly learned.

Another side of normal human life also died in Siberia confirming what they had been told on arrival. There appeared to be no romantic or sexual interest in the camp probably as a result of the combination of exhaustion, illness, hunger and cold.

Transport in the area was primitive. There were only dirt tracks, no proper roads at all. When the winter snows came, the deportees were told to trample down the snow and make temporary new tracks. People couldn't run because you couldn't breathe if you did. It was so cold the lungs couldn't take in much of the icy air. It was a very dry cold which threatened to choke you if you breathed too deeply.

Snow drifted feet thick. Jan said the cold didn't bother him, that he just walked fast from place to place. But he was working indoors much of the time so was spared continual cold. The building the family stayed in was made of very thick timber, and with a fire inside, it felt quite warm.

They were paid every ten days; Sunday was not recognised as a day of rest nor was the Christian calendar observed. Their earnings were used to buy necessities such as food grown by the local villagers. In the three to four months of spring and summer the local people managed to grow a lot of produce, including fruit and vegetables.

When asked about meat Danka responded,

'Do I remember any meat? I don't think so, maybe once or twice. Must have been chicken.'

There were no books at all, and little paper but Danka kept a record of spending and noted on paper the sale of a duvet in Charytonowo.

The little money Jan and Zosia earned could also be used to buy from the local shop within the barracks: bread, sometimes oatmeal, very occasionally a rare treat such as sugar cubes, but this, when available, was rationed to 200 grams per family. Due to the lack of fresh fruit scurvy was rampant in the first months before summer came.

Once Jan felt more settled in the camp he had a few conversations with the NKVD people in the joinery workshop. They were educated, intelligent people, not harsh or sadistic but they knew their role was to obey orders so there was an unspoken understanding.

There were few work casualties even amongst those who worked all year on hard labour outside in the cold though one day one of Jan's friends fell into the swollen river in summer and drowned. The unusually good safety record probably reflected the priorities of the local commandant. Deaths meant less labourers, more burials, more paperwork.

The commandant was Ukrainian, a descendent of a group of deportees sent there in the previous century. He was not oppressive. Rather he was as tolerant and kind towards his captives as his position allowed.

The family were allowed to send letters, postcard-style to their family. Unthinkingly at first they described their ordeal which meant that the letters were not delivered, having been scrutinised by a local censor. However eventually some got through. These were delivered by the Red Cross. In return they started to receive parcels from Lwow from Janina's sister Irena. People were allowed to receive only one parcel a month from a particular individual but there was no limit to how many individuals could send a parcel. Once this was known the family got the message out and more parcels arrived, sent under the names of friends or servants of their relatives. Another rule stated that you had to be able to name the person who was sending you the parcel, this in order to prevent people sending more than one under false names.

Danka was always the one who went to the office to see if any parcels had arrived. She wasn't working, and the commandant liked her spirit. When a new parcel had arrived and Danka couldn't guess the name of the person who sent it the commandant started spelling the name letter by letter so that Danka could guess it, otherwise she wouldn't have been able to get the parcel.

The family never experienced, saw or heard of physical or sexual abuse, nor any form of psychological or emotional abuse in the time they spent in Siberia. There was no sadistic behaviour from the officials, unlike the legion of horrific stories recounted by those Poles sent to other Soviet or German camps. The NKVD administrators at Charytonowo were normal people, and decent. Similarly the family was unaware of any stealing between the Poles, or between Poles and the local people.

Younger children like Danka were spared heavy work and encouraged to go to 'school'. Janina refused to allow Danka to go to the school, saying that Danka had already finished her primary education. Janina was scared that her youngest daughter might be brainwashed into believing the atheistic, communist, anti-Polish propaganda that was being directed at the children.

There was a cinema for prisoners, but it too showed only Soviet propaganda. Children were tempted to go with the reward of chocolate for sale at very low prices, so some families allowed their children to go in order to help ease their hunger.

On Easter Sunday 1940 some of the Poles decided to secretly celebrate with a religious and patriotic service in their hut and had invited families from the other huts to join them, something strictly forbidden by camp rules. The punishment was extremely severe, possibly even death. The commandant came to learn of this secret religious ceremony. Instead of waiting until everyone was in the barracks then rounding them up, he marched between all the barracks shouting deliberately loudly that he was coming to inspect. This was his warning to all the people inside celebrating Easter to leave and return to their own barracks before he got near them. From then the Poles knew they could say prayers together in safety but had to be careful to keep the commandant happy with their behaviour in every way so that his life could be as easy as possible.

Not compelled either to work or to go to school, Danka and other children went down to the river each day to collect broken branches and smaller logs and take them back to the barracks. Larger logs were dragged back. They would cut them up and use them for firewood. Everyone contributed as best they could to ensure the survival of all. But despite the fairness of the camp commander three major threats existed, for the local people as well as the recent arrivals. These were malnutrition, disease and winter.

The following excerpts from a letter by Janina to Wladyslaw, dated 22 May 1940, contain the first written record we have from the family while they lived in the labour camp. It was kept after Wladyslaw's death by his two sisters, for Janina and the children should they survive the war and ever return to Haczow. This and other precious mementoes of these years were given to Danka on her first return to Poland in 1964.

"… [Janina's brother] Henryk wrote from Lwow. He thought you'd have received a letter from him by now explaining what happened to us. Everybody is alive but I'm already down to 50kg."

Prior to the war Janina weighed around 75kg so she had lost almost a third of her weight in just three months.

"…We were taken away on 10 February and arrived at this camp on 10 March. We are 450km from Archangel on the River Wyzgyda. My sister in law and Dobrusia are with us. I can't write everything because you can imagine the situation here. How are you? I hope you are OK."

All letters from the camps were censored, so many were not delivered because of their contents. It is surprising how many did get through from Janina and the children to Wladyslaw in Haczow. It is harder to imagine his response to these few letters from his wife and children, hard to understand how his mind raced to understand what was not written, what was deemed best to be left unsaid. Hard also to imagine Wladyslaw wondering whether the intervening weeks between the date on the letters and the day he received them had gone well for his family. Anything might have happened in those weeks. Were they even still alive by the time he read the letter?

The same is true for the letters the family received from Wladyslaw. With what joy might the children have responded to the few words from their absent father. How well did he hide his illness, or his fears for their wellbeing and for the fate of Poland, lying under the totalitarian oppression of both Hitler and Stalin?

But at least one positive thing was certain. Spring and summer, no matter how brief, were coming to Charytonowo.

Summer at Charytonowo

May to August 1940

In May families of Jews from the area of Poland where the Stepeks had lived started to arrive at the labour camp in Charytonowo. Around that time the first early season berries also started to appear. Danka and Zosia went out together to pick the berries, eating as many as they could, saving some for Janina and Jan and started to sell the rest to the Jewish arrivals. They quickly worked out the going rate: one rouble for a glass of blueberries. Sometimes twenty roubles from better off Russians who saw the children as people in need. Some also swapped salted fish for blueberries.

This new variety of food helped ease the scurvy that had so afflicted the detainees. Bilberries had been the first to appear and proved a real godsend. It also gave Danka a greater sense of purpose, a way in which she could help the family in their primary aim, to survive.

As a child Danka had been ill several times in Poland and while recovering in bed she read a lot of the books which Wladyslaw and Janina had in the house. Some were medical books and from this she learned which mushrooms were safe and which were poisonous. As she said decades later,

"In Russia there were so many different kinds of mushrooms. Big mushrooms, hollow inside. Are they safe? Yes. Sticky mushrooms but good for you."

From the local people she learned to stir a pond to make it so muddy that the fish would have to stick their heads out of the water to breathe. As they came to the surface Danka caught them.

Later in the summer the children found big red berries growing out of the mud. Though Danka never found out their name the locals confirmed they were safe to eat. An abundance of blueberries grew through much of the summer, followed by raspberries and cranberries. Janina went picking too and this helped her poor health for the time being. They filled buckets each day which they would sell to people who passed alongside the camp on cargo and passenger boats, exchanging them for roubles or bread. Danka always ran to try to be first to get to the boats so she could sell all her berries. The amount of people on boats going up and downstream grew substantially in those summer months.

A second letter from Charytonowo survives, dated 18 August 1940, written by Janina to Wladyslaw. It reflects these changes in their circumstances but Janina also looks ahead to when summer ends with a sense of foreboding. Who knows how many weeks or months of summer's blessings they had before winter arrived. When Janina wrote the letter it was around a year since Wladyslaw had last seen his family.

The letter gives a rare insight into the fears and grief of Janina in those summer months in the Soviet Union's labour camp system.

"Oh my dearest! We received your letter of 7 July luckily. All of us are still alive. There are now lots of berries and mushrooms so we are eating them and some we're selling. Somehow we're managing but what will winter make of us; will we still be alive after that? All of us are barefoot and the winter lasts eight months and starts in two months' time. I don't know how we will manage with that. We're missing everybody but life has to go on. I could write quite a lot but we can't write about everything. It's such a good thing that you know where we are. Henrik and his family were taken away to Russia as well. We don't have any news of them. Gutek Konopnicki [Janina's nephew] is in Russia as well. Irena [Janina's sister and Gutek's mother] is in Lwow. She is having to get through her tragedy alone [her husband was shot dead by the Russians when he was trying to cross the border with Gutek into Romania to rejoin the Polish troops. He was a major. Gutek lied that he was only 16 so instead of being shot he was taken to Russia.] Please don't forget about us and try to get us out of here. Send best wishes to Czsiek's family [another of Janina's brothers, living in Krosno, near Haczow. One of his sons disappeared during the war]

Janina"

In the neighbouring villages all the men were engine drivers or had skilled work experience maintaining the railway while the women worked on the collective farm, primarily looking after cows. Danka by this time had become quite well known by the locals for her energetic foraging and bartering of berries and goods sent from Poland by family and friends. As a result she was asked if she would look after a local woman's child while the mother worked on the farm. She received a glass of milk and a slice of bread for this, two treasured sources of nutrition. One day the woman gave Danka a piece of material for a dress, which Danka made. Later in their odyssey Danka would exchange the dress for something of greater urgency.

The family experienced the famous white nights, where darkness never came, but this was not the enjoyable experience that tourists today travel thousands of miles to witness. Instead it came as exhaustion set in for the workers logging the trees or dragging the timbers down to the riverside well into the eerily lit night time.

Still, this was a time of hope for the family. They had made it through the horrendous journey and the first, most dangerous, winter. Janina, though weaker and now underweight, found some hope in the fact that they had begun to dry and store food for the long winter ahead. Wladyslaw was alive, and they were in touch with each other. The three children, although worryingly thin, seemed healthy and strong. Moreover, they seemed mentally robust and if anything, more resilient than they had ever been. By the end of August 1940, they had survived six months in the camp. How would they fare, braced for their first full winter in the frozen north of Russia?

Winter at Charytonowo

September 1940 to April 1941

The family had learned quickly from the locals. They saved many of the berries they collected in the summer and autumn, storing them in barrels and keeping them cold in the remaining snowy areas until wintertime. So when winter arrived the family would melt the berries as and when needed and help prevent the return of scurvy. Although this good fortune meant there was enough for the Stepeks, many in the camp fell prey to night blindness because of a lack of vitamins and minerals, and this condition hampered their vision even as daylight came. This was a severe handicap as daylight lasted only four to six hours and they had to work for their food and earnings in that short time. If they couldn't work, they didn't earn. If they didn't earn, they received no food.

Not everyone was fortunate. All of one family consisting of sixteen people died in the camp from malnutrition followed by the onset of disease. The malnutrition meant that their bodies were less able to withstand the diseases when they came. Many people died in this way, and with winter coming the fears increased. Moreover although few ever saw them, the sound of wolves howling in hunger could be heard in the camp every night, and the traditional European fear of wolves as narrated in so many folk tales added to the underlying dread of what winter would bring.

The long winter months from September 1940 to April 1941 became a matter of willing the body to stay warm despite the omnipresent cold when outside, and to demand that the mind remain hopeful despite the seemingly endless darkness that pervaded. Each day became a monotonous ritual of carefully rationed dried food that they had stored, shorter but more intense work for Jan and Zosia, care and rest when any of the family fell ill. An essential task was fuelling the wooden stove to keep warm in the barracks that was their home, and the welcome but all too brief forgetfulness of sleep. Christmas came and went with little cheer and only symbolic gifts such as an extra piece of dried fruit was given.

1940 gave way to 1941. A New Year appeared, seemingly devoid of hope for the family and for Poland. A long bleak period followed that seemed to last forever.

Then as if by magic one morning spring appeared to the people of Charytonowo, sunlight with a tinge of warmth, a less icy feel in the wind. And with spring hope too became alive again. They had survived the eight months of Russia's iconic winter.

Last Months at Charytonowo

May to September 1941

In the spring of 1941 Danka discovered more types of mushrooms. They were growing deeper in the forest. Danka by this time had become expert on the subject; she knew which mushrooms were edible. The forest area was very flat and muddy and one could easily sink in the mud so usually they would walk along the railway line to stay safe and not get lost. It was easy to get lost as the forests stretched for hundreds of miles. Once lost the chances of finding the camp were minimal. In all likelihood the wolves would put an end to you.

That same spring the commandant informed the Polish families that if they had money to pay for it from their meagre earnings, they could rent land for their own use and even build a home on it. The latter was inconceivable but they could afford to rent some land from the money earned by Jan and Zosia. So the family planted potatoes that spring. The soil was very sandy and remarkably fertile in those few months of sunshine and warmth. Everything grew so fast. The forms of life had adapted to a region where winter started to appear in late September and from November till April the temperature was usually around minus thirty-eight degrees Centigrade. Those potatoes were to prove more valuable than gold.

First though they had to prepare the ground. In the field allocated to them they first cut down the trees. Then they put thick pieces of timber into the soil under the roots of the trees and jumped on the timber to use as a lever to dislodge the long roots of the trees. They exchanged a duvet for potatoes from one of the local people and planted the potatoes. Once harvested a few months later they dried the potatoes in a sack to keep them for the long winter that was to come. Occasionally Danka would sneak into a nearby field to dig up and steal turnips. Some of this too they dried for winter.

Until the summer of 1941 the family received parcels from the farmhands and servants at home. Danka was given the responsibility to open these and decide what was best to keep for immediate use, what would be stored for a later date, and what could be bartered for other essentials from the local people.

The following letter was written to Wladyslaw in Zosia's handwriting but signed by both girls.

18 May 1941

Dearest father!

I am very sorry that you are not getting any news from us although we have sent lots of letters. We are getting lots of letters from you. The last letter from 14 April and from 27 April. We are feeling all right except mama is not very well.

Janek and I are working. Janek is working in joinery making furniture and I'm working on the river sorting out the timber. My work is not very heavy and I'm earning five roubles a day. Janek's wages are getting better. They are taking 10% of our wages and Janek is paying more because he is earning more. Please don't worry about us. We managed to live over the winter and we're still alive. And at summer it will be easier. The spring is rather late. We are hoping to plant some potatoes and are preparing the field. Please write to us often because we are missing you and we will try to write so that our letters will reach you. We send to you and aunts all our kisses and best.

Zosia and Danuta.

The princely sum of five roubles that Zosia mentions in her letter was able to buy two small loaves of dark rye bread - if any was available. Although the letters to Wladyslaw were self-censored in order to ensure that they were delivered, it appears that many had gone astray.

The Red Cross were doing an astonishing job of getting letters from Wladyslaw to his family and Wladyslaw was writing at least every fortnight some fifteen months after the deportation. However, he was unwell, and plotting in the underground army in the midst of a cruel occupation, so finding the time to write and to be as positive as possible for the sake of his family, must have been a real struggle. Some of his friends, neighbours and colleagues from Haczow had by this time been arrested and sent to Auschwitz where thirteen residents of Haczow died.

The most poignant part of the letter is the phrase "except Mama is not very well." This must have been as explicit a statement that the girls felt would be considered acceptable by the censors. Danka said later that her mother was a broken woman even before the deportation and that her health and weight plummeted further as time went on in the camp.

Yet Zosia's spirit inhabits the letter. The determination to survive, the positive case that Jan and she were working and earning, that food was available to them and that in the summer there was promise of more food from the planting that they were planning at the time of writing.

Then came a seismic, historic shift. On 22 June 1941 Germany tore up its pact of mutual non-aggression with the Soviet Union and invaded Soviet-occupied Poland with the intention of conquering Russia in Blitzkrieg style before winter set in.

As a result, without knowing the reason things worsened for the detainees in Charytonowo. After completing his carpentry work Jan had to help the loggers, pushing the huge, felled tree trunks into the river. He was effectively working around the clock, guided by the Arctic night time sunlight.

The German invasion was completely unexpected and caused chaos in the Soviet Union. There was a sudden war mobilisation. The communication systems were inadequate and ineffective, particularly in the most distant regions of a country as huge as Russia. Therefore, the Poles at Charytonowo did not hear about the invasion for several weeks.

When they found out there was great consternation. What would happen to them? What would happen to their families in Poland? As they were absorbing this momentous change in the war, in late August, another piece of news arrived, and it was simply stunning.

They were informed that on July 30 representatives of the Polish Government-in-Exile and Stalin had signed an agreement for mutual aid in the war against Hitler, which included an "amnesty for Polish citizens deprived of freedom on Soviet territory". As part of this agreement Polish armed forces would be formed in southern Russia, under General Wladyslaw Anders, newly released from a Moscow prison in which he had been tortured. Those freed under the amnesty would be eligible to join this new army.

The Polish camp residents were told that they could leave. The camp commander asked them to stay, arguing that winter was not far off, and that although their lives were hard in the camp, they at least had somewhere to sleep at night. Who knew, he said, what tribulations would beset them if they set off on the two-thousand-mile journey south to try to find Polish recruitment centres?

The Stepeks took this warning seriously. They feared that with Janina already severely weakened they wouldn't manage through the winter if they left. Within days of the announcement, Danka, still only 14, caught pneumonia so immediate flight was impossible.

Jan's friend Wladek Wasco had been deported to the same camp along with his parents and brothers. This family, along with almost all the rest of the Maczkowce population, decided to leave as soon as the notice came through that the Poles were free to depart the camp.

Within a week or two of the departure of their friends and neighbours from Maczkowce, news came that the Germans were already nearing Moscow. This made the Stepeks review their decision to stay for the time being. They wanted to be beyond Moscow before it was cut off by the Nazis.

Janina sold most of what remained of their possessions from Poland – duvets, clothes - and with the money bought train tickets which authorised them to go as far south as Crimea, well past the agreed but vague area of southern Russia that they were supposed to travel to. She remembered from her farming purchases in Poland that many fruits and vegetables imported from Russia were marked Crimea. So she reasoned that in case they couldn't find the Polish armed forces gathering in the south, they at least could get to somewhere warm and healthy.

By the time Danka was well and they decided to leave the camp it was almost deserted. On September 11 they left by boat along the River Wyczygda just before it froze over for the winter. Where the Wyczygda meets the River Dwyna ice was already forming. What awaited them was a long journey into the unknown, with both winter and the German army snapping at their heels, sickness and hunger as real possibilities, and the tantalising possibility of freedom from the Soviet Union and protection under the care of Polish officers.

Wladyslaw

March 1940 to September 1941

Wladyslaw's activities and feelings while apart from his family
are mostly unknown, sparse and often circumstantial.

After being taken to a railway station in September 1939 he
managed to make it back to Haczow undetected by the Red
Army and the German forces. He was welcomed back by his
sisters and old friends from the village and surrounding towns
and despite being seriously unwell he joined the resistance, or
Armia Krajowa. Because of his ill-health most of his activities
consisted of thinking and planning activities against the
occupying German Army.

Exactly when the news reached him that his family and the
whole population of Maczkowce had been taken from their
home is unknown. It is likely that this news arrived some time
before he became aware of where they were taken. Clearly
even normal mailing services would have been severely
disrupted by the war, let alone postal communications
between German-occupied Poland and the far north of
Russia.

By 20 September 1940, a full year after he had to flee his
home, Wladyslaw was fully aware of his family's plight in
Archangel. When he discovered what had happened to his
family Wladyslaw wrote a letter intended for the German

embassy in Moscow, in which he requested their assistance in freeing his family from Siberia. There are two versions of this letter; the original handwritten draft, and a typed copied in German. This was during the period from September 1939 until June 1941 when the Germans and Soviets had a pact of mutual non-aggression. However he was uncertain whether or not to send it, so consulted with his relations. He concluded that it was better not to send it, because it may backfire and place the family in worse danger. If they were released and sent back to German-occupied Poland Jan would be conscripted into the German army and sent to the frontline, and Zosia and Danka may be sent to do forced labour in Germany. Worse, it might put a spotlight on the family as potential troublemakers in the eyes of the Soviet authorities. Wladyslaw therefore had to make a terrible decision, to leave the fate of his entire family to chance.

Another letter exists from him dated December 1942, sent from Krakow to his sisters in Haczow. In it he explains that he has been diagnosed with a form of bowel cancer and that an operation in the city has been proposed. He therefore asks his sisters to forward him his ration cards so that he might still be able to survive while away from Haczow. The fact that Wladyslaw didn't have to explain to his sisters why he went to Krakow suggests that they already knew that he was going to a specialist doctor in the city. It also tells us either that he was still living with his sisters at the time or they knew where he

was living locally and so knew where they could obtain his
ration cards.

His daughter Danka had been told some decades later that
Wladyslaw was treated further at the spa town of Zakopane.
He died on 26th June 1943 and was buried in Haczow where
his headstone still stands. Danka was told that he died in
Zakopane but his death certificate says he died in Haczow.

It is likely that he never learned what became of his wife
and children after they left the labour camp at Charytonowo
some twenty months or so before his death. He may not even
have learned that they had been released and were trying to
reach freedom.

A tragic end had come to one who had fought for Poland's
freedom twice in his short life. He had tried in his own way to
help create a sense of common purpose amongst the various
minorities in the Polish republic before the war. He believed
in social democracy and in multiculturalism.

It is a blessing that he did not live to see the mass ethnic
expulsions that erupted in Poland in the post-war period, nor
the failure of his homeland to reimpose a democratic
government. Everything he believed in and strove for in
Poland was utterly destroyed and was not to be restored for
over half a century.

Odyssey

September 1941 to January 1942

Janina was clear. They should head to Crimea. Food for the family was her priority. Moreover she knew Crimea was far to the warmer south and that it was on the sea. Both of these features spoke of health and recovery. This was Danka's recollection of her mother's thinking at the time.

Jan remembered things differently. He too spoke of the family selling virtually everything they had made or bought in the barracks: a little furniture which Jan had made, clothes, bric-a-brac, anything anyone would buy. But he remembers the family considering the Middle East as a route to escape, with Tashkent, now capital of Uzbekistan, a first target to reach. But even that was over two thousand miles away.

Realistically though their first goal was to return to Kotlas, the first major town south-west of Charytonowo. Privately Jan was pessimistic at this point. He thought it likely that they would perish in the Soviet Union and it didn't really matter if they died in Charytonowo or some other part of Russia, but now that they had agreed a nearby destination to aim for, they made light of the difficulties they might face on their journey further on in the journey.

Not far from Charytonowo they were met by some Polish officers assigned to help the deportees as much as they could.

These officers were probably detainees newly released by the terms of the amnesty and by chance had been imprisoned in the region. With their help they managed to reach Kotlas in just four days, spending two days on sledges followed by a goods train which was heading to Kotlas. At the first station they stopped at there was hot soup ready for sale made by the locals. Thus the first part of the journey was achieved without too many privations. They were even invited to join the Polish officers assigned to them for dinner in a restaurant but that sense of security and luxury did not last.

On arrival at Kotlas the family worried how they were to continue the journey south to Crimea. It quickly became clear that having rail tickets was a cruel joke. Visions of an orderly migration evaporated in the mass crowds of Polish and other deportees waiting at Kotlas, and as they were soon to discover, the same chaotic situation existed at dozens of stations as they travelled further south. The railway station was completely crammed with Poles desperate to reach the Polish troops in the south. It started to become apparent to the family how shocking had been the scale of the deportations from Poland.

For three days they waited but no trains came other than those filled with goods and military personnel. On one of these days Danka found herself standing and looking enviously into the window of a small café, where one man sat eating soup and bread. The man noticed Danka and came outside and gave her some of his soup and bread. Danka remembered the Russian people in Kotlas as kind and helpful during those three difficult days.

All of the Poles at Kotlas seemed to be in much the same situation as the Stepeks. Their limited means had all but come to an end so they had to survive on their wits. They fed themselves by barter or theft. Unlike the Russian workers they came across, the Poles had no ration cards so it was hard for them to obtain the bare minimum amount of food to keep going even if they had money. Bread was such a rarity in Kotlas it was used as unofficial currency. One loaf would buy a packet of tobacco. If you had bread and tobacco you could buy traditional shoes made of felt, boots or a pipe.

Eventually NKVD officers forced them onto cattle trains similar to the ones they had endured nineteen months previously. Thus Janina's earlier purchase of train tickets to Crimea had turned out to be a complete waste of money. However they were just glad to be on transport taking them further away from the camp and hopefully nearer to Polish authorities. The timing was another worrying factor: it was winter already and every day would make conditions harder for travel.

The train travelled south towards Moscow but as German forces progressed swiftly towards the capital the train was redirected eastwards by the NKVD officials in charge. This took them in the direction of the Ural mountains.

So many people boarded the train at various stopping points, official and unofficial, that it was impossible for officials to check for tickets so no one was hindered from travelling by a lack of resources. At the stopping places wood was taken from bed boards in empty dwellings and used to make fires for warmth and cooking if there was food. Sometimes the desperate travellers would risk breaking up abandoned railway carriages but this was a criminal offence. It had been said that Russian soldiers would not hesitate to shoot people who were caught committing such a crime.

During these early weeks, with little money and only a few possessions left to barter or exchange, the family relied upon the potatoes they had grown in their little plot of land in the camp. They also had the mushrooms picked by Danka. These had been dried to preserve them for food to help see them through the winter, which they had expected to spend at the camp. Janina had baked the potatoes in the oven so that they became hard like crisps. With these bare ingredients and water from snow they melted, they were able to make soup in the cattle wagon which was now their home.

The only other food consisted of a porridge made of bread which was first crumbled and boiled in melted snow. Large quantities of snow were melted for drinking and for cooking and washing. The station water taps were invariably frozen so this ritual of gathering and melting snow was to keep thousands alive through the long journey south.

After passing through the eastern outskirts of Moscow conditions improved a little when the large group the Stepeks were with was joined by a group of Ukrainian refugees seeking to escape from the German advance by travelling east into Asia. The two groups worked together to find food, wood for burning, and to collect snow for water. They shared everything. Jan met three young Poles aged around twenty also at this time. They suggested the idea of posing as Ukrainians, believing that they might be treated more favourably by Russian officials if they thought the Poles were Ukrainian. So the family tried this while in the wider Moscow area but there was no way of knowing in hindsight whether or not it produced any better results.

The area surrounding Moscow was in total chaos. Thousands of civilians were getting onto trains to all destinations. The Stepek family did the same, taking any train that headed east, to get as far from the German forces as possible.

The winter of 1941 had arrived early, and the cold and damp were becoming more intense for the refugees. The full bitter onslaught to come was anticipated with dread. At one stop when the cold had become unbearable and there was no wood for heat Jan worked with a small group to chop down a telegraph pole which bordered the railway track. This was a major crime which was considered an act of sabotage. Whilst in the midst of this act they were spotted by a guard who opened fire. Jan managed to jump into the gap between two wagons and dived into the one the family was in through its half-open door. The guards never searched for him.

In some respects the journey from Siberia in cattle trucks mirrored their original deportation from Maczkowce though this time there were no guards overseeing their every move. Sometimes they could see nearby local villages from their frequent stopping points. Some of the Poles risked going to these to beg or barter despite the possibility that the train might set off again without them.

On one of these expeditions Jan was arrested by an NKVD guard. Jan had been at a black market looking for provisions, so he was taken by the guard to the local commissar. Pretending that he was confident and unafraid Jan told the commissar in fluent Russian that he was part of a party of patriots on their way to join the army and that the transport wouldn't leave without him. This would mean that up to three thousand army recruits would be stranded as a result of his decision to arrest Jan. These recruits, he continued, were needed for Russian urgent efforts to halt the German advance. He suggested that the commissar might even face the death penalty for his actions and that he should consider the consequences carefully. Unsure whether his suggestions had any truth in it or not, the commissar decided not to risk the worst-case scenario and released him.

Their troubles increased. Cold and gnawing hunger were constant enemies as supplies of food and wood became increasingly difficult to find. They resorted to desperate measures. They made raids on other trains, including one train loaded with tea for Uzbekistan. They drank that tea for weeks. On another occasion a guard dog belonging to an NKVD guard disappeared and couldn't be found despite prolonged searches. Jan, together with some of the group, desperate in their hunger, had captured and eaten it.

Around the turn of 1941 to 1942, thirty roubles which Jan had managed to save was stolen. This was the only money the family still had, kept aside to be used only in the most desperate moments of need through the rest of their journey. Now they had lost it.

The journey continued through snow covered tracks surrounded by virgin forests of pine, spruce and occasionally birch. These stretched as far as the eye could see day after day as they travelled. The snow was pure and soft, untouched by any human but the beauty was lost on those who viewed it all. They were sustained only by the thought that they were slowly heading towards their destination, and that Polish army corps would be waiting for them as had been promised. There they would know food, hot baths and security again, under the care of their own people. Though morbid thoughts crept into his frequent optimistic dreams, Jan wondered if they would reach their destination. Everyone lived with the gnawing terror that their train would stop at a siding to have the engine removed because it was needed elsewhere. They had heard these stories from other refugees and local people wherever they went, of abandoned trains filled with people still locked inside, completely forgotten, all left to die in the middle of this never-ending landscape.

Jan worried that the snow might drift and cover the train any time it was stuck in a siding, and would never be found. Everyone would die of cold and starvation over a matter of days, weeks, even months. A slow, tortuous end. Eventually they'd be found, and their frozen bodies thrown into the snow. The wolves and crows would rip their bodies apart. Their families and friends in Poland would never know where or how they died. How many millions already lay along this beautiful endless plain? Jan wondered.

This was not just fantasy dreamed up in the midst of hunger and cold and endless journeying. Sometimes on the way they would pass trains in sidings covered with snow. Their contents could only be guessed at. Most likely they would be machinery, arms for the war, flour or cereals, which the weather had conspired to keep from the people. But there could be hundreds of people, long dead. The silence only made it seem more possible.

Each time they were put into a siding in order to let other trains pass, the impact of the buffers bumping into one another caused great fear in the train. Perhaps the impact was caused by the engine being removed. Sometimes the delay in the siding went on for days and time ceased to exist. These things happened simply because the Germans were pushing south to conquer the oil lands in Kazakhstan, so vast swathes of people from western Russia were escaping southwards and eastwards. This meant the trains and wagons carrying Polish citizens towards Kazakhstan were cluttering up the rail system. They were in the way. They were not a priority at a time of great crisis for the Soviet Union. There were far too many trains on the tracks at the same time in the same regions.

Also, unexpectedly, there were too many people in the same region at the same time. As a result there was an even greater shortage of food than usual. People were fleeing from Moscow, from everywhere threatened by the German onslaught resulting in there being not enough supplies to feed the number of people and keep them sheltered and warm.

The sight of the Ural mountains, stretching for two thousand miles, was an awesome sight for Jan. There, at Swerdlowsk (in the far east of present-day Ukraine) they remained for four days on the train, then moved east. In doing so the Stepek family left Europe and entered Asia for the first time in their lives. Long stops at stations continued as did the bitterness of the cold and the constant presence of hunger.

Trains they were on came to their destination and all the refugees had to disembark and hope that another train going in the right direction would come along. This happened dozens of times over a matter of weeks. When not on a train they slept whenever and wherever they could and took any new passing train going in the rough general direction, south if possible, but east was also an option. The problem was that often a train would appear and the driver would tell them the name of the destination but no one knew where it was in relation to where the Stepeks were aiming to reach. They were barely surviving the journey, and long periods of fatalism caused by fatigue swept over the family.

Jan lived each moment as it arose with barely a thought for the future. He daydreamed as a means of escape. His recurring thought was to survive. I will survive. I will survive this. Occasionally his thoughts would drift ahead trying to visualise what the next few days would bring. He wandered in his thoughts through the literature he had read at school; literary portrayals of the Russian Revolution, descriptions of people dying in St Petersburg. He wondered if their situation was what he was now experiencing. Decades later, watching the film Doctor Zhivago, Jan commented that the scenes in that movie of long harrowing journeys on trains during the revolution was very similar to what the family had endured.

The deprivation continued. More cold, more hunger, continual stops for days at snow covered stations or in vast open spaces; it made them feel they were in an unworldly ghost train travelling endlessly in time and space with no ultimate destination.

Unknown to the family, the train was taking them further and further east. The first sign they saw, in late November, some two months after they had set out, was as they passed the central-eastern Kazakh city of Karaganda, near Astana. But at the time the family had no idea where this was, nor did any of their fellow refugees. They all still thought they were heading due south but were now almost as far from where they wanted to be as when they started their journey only this time they were too far east instead of too far north.

A few days later someone told them that they were not too far from the Chinese border, travelling just north of the Himalayas. They had no idea if this was true but it was grim news, and to make matters worse it was bitterly cold once more.

On the sixth of December 1941 the cattle truck which the Stepeks had climbed into was stuck in yet another railway siding. There were hundreds of exhausted Poles crammed inside, hungry and ill. They had few if any resources, and their energy was nearly spent.

Janina by this stage of their ordeal was unable to stand without help and could not walk for more than a few seconds. She was increasingly sick, worn out, and starving. The family

147

hadn't eaten for a week and were surviving by melting the snow from the ground and the icicles that formed all day long on their cattle train, these being their only sources of water.

After several hours of forlorn waiting another train stopped on the track adjacent. It was filled with Russians fleeing the advancing German forces in the west. The Polish refugees, aching with hunger, ran out to beg from the Russian people on the other train. Many Russians generously shared food with them.

Danka watched this dramatic scene from the open door which had been slid open by Jan. He and Zosia had gone begging, leaving Danka to look after their mother. They returned empty handed and the whole family sank into silent desolation.

Then Danka thought she heard a word that sounded something like 'Dyevotchka'. It was hard to hear amongst the bustle of Polish beggars and Russians. Again she heard it, only this time much more clearly. A woman's voice. "Devochka" – Russian for "girl".

She started to look for the woman following the direction from which the word had come. A Russian woman, wrapped in a thick fur coat and hat was standing at the door of the other train, almost directly opposite Danka's carriage. Danka stared at her, ready to see what she might be able to beg from the lady, an opportunity to show again what her innocent looks might draw from a stranger.

The woman was young, maybe thirty years old, and to Danka's eyes she looked beautiful. She stared back and smiled at Danka. Then, without a word, she delved into a bag at her side and threw something large and heavy straight at Danka. Instinctively Danka recoiled but she caught the object. It was a very large loaf of bread. She looked up to thank the lady, but she had already gone back into the carriage.

This loaf fed the family for a week. They had nothing else during that time, and it is likely that without it they would all have died of hunger.

The date was the sixth of December, St Nicholas's day. It is the day that in some parts of Poland children receive an early Christmas present.

It would be wonderful to know who this woman was who saved the family in this way. Janina's children, grandchildren and great grandchildren all owe their lives to her. Several other strangers had already helped them, and many more were to do so as their odyssey continued. It is due to the altruism of these people that this branch of the Stepek line survived. Of all human traits it is this, the kindness of strangers, especially in the most trying of times, which is most moving. It is surely our greatest attribute and source of hope.

Hours, maybe days passed. Then just as suddenly as it had stopped, the train started again. It seemed to Jan that it was changing direction again and heading west. There seemed no sense or consistency in the direction the train was heading. The family ran out of food again, and there were no supplies to be had. The train was continually put into sidings to allow convoys of military trains to pass. Hundreds of other trains full of people, Polish, Russian, ethnic minorities of the Soviet Union, were still fleeing from the war, so the train system remained chaotic. Janina spent almost the entire journey lying on a wooden bench, slowly fading away from hunger and the thoughts in her head of the torture she had endured for so long.

January came. A new year. They had survived four months of travel and the life was sinking out of everyone on the train, their spirits almost vanquished. Then at last, like a miracle out of the blue the train stopped at a real town. No. A city. They were in Tashkent, Uzbekistan. Tashkent, 1724 miles from Kotlas as the crow flies, but with the constant changes of direction they must have travelled double that distance.

No one had any energy left to show even a spark of interest even though they had reached their main destination. The starving do not celebrate redemption. Often they die on being freed from their plight, because resisting death was the only thing that had been keeping them alive.

The train the family had taken on this last long stage of their journey had been crammed, perhaps carrying four or five hundred people. By the time they arrived at Tashkent around half had died. Corpses had been taken out of the train every time they had stopped. The dead were mostly babies, young children and the elderly.

Part 4: Refugees

Polito-Oddiet, Kazakhstan

January to April 1942

On disembarking at Tashkent everyone was loaded onto carts and sent to various temporary centres. The Stepek family were allocated to a village inhabited by various nationalities, but mostly comprising Uzbeks, Kazakhs, and some Russians. Connected to the village was a collective farm comprising all the fields surrounding the settlement. The main crop was cotton. There were other fields lying empty, the vegetables which grew there having been harvested months earlier.

The Stepek family were told they each had to pick 20kg of cotton per day if they were to earn the reward of enough food to keep them from hunger. Danka could only manage 8kg at best so her wages amounted to 100g of flour and half a pancake. Janina couldn't stand unaided let alone work so it was down to Jan and Zosia to pick enough cotton to keep the family from starvation.

Two weeks later they were moved again. This journey entailed fourteen days of travel during which they were given no food at all, nor could they barter or beg for anything en route.

The settlement to which they were delivered was referred to as Polito by Danka in a handwritten report she was later to write, and as Polit-Oddiet by Zosia in her later notes on the

153

subject. Zosia notes that it was in Kazakhstan whereas Jan in an interview suggested it was in Uzbekistan.

When Danka was asked what she thought of that place her first words were "Oh God, scorpions".

The family heard from other Poles news for the first time that the Polish army had set up a recruitment centre somewhere in the region. Jan was anxious to learn if he would be able to enlist in the army, but he had no way of knowing how to reach such a centre if indeed it existed.

The family were housed in the corner of a mud hut. Lack of food continued to be their greatest crisis. As a family they were given a total of 200 grams of flour each day, plus a half-litre of milk. In the first week they were also given a sack containing 200 grams of dried apples. Jan added to this meagre amount by stealing cabbage and potatoes from the nearby fields. The cabbages were invariably frozen but were devoured immediately. Occasionally they were able to obtain some rice. The local people were in a similar position of malnutrition. Now they had a stream of hungry refugees to add to the mouths needing fed. Feelings ranged from anger on all sides, to a reluctant acceptance of the situation, to unimaginable kindness from some of the locals. Everyone was hungry, constantly thinking of food, and, asleep at night Zosia would dream of eating the varieties of food they ate back in Poland.

The family were again allocated work collecting cotton. Janina was still unable to contribute, as her weakness and illness had worsened still. For their work Jan, Zosia and Danka were given a soup which was mostly water with a few grains of rice in it.

The nearest town was 30km away but none of the family had the energy to walk there, nor any reason as they had no money with which to buy food.

One day Jan was summoned to go a nearby village to the local office of the NKVD. He found himself facing a commissar sitting at a table. On the table was a gun and a piece of bread.

The official asked Jan to sit down.

"Which of these do you want?" said the commissar.

Jan said he didn't want to play word games.

"Say what you mean."

The commissar said "We have a common enemy. The Germans. As a Pole you should be on our side. If not, then you are against us. Work alongside us and we'll share our bread with you. Refuse, and you get the gun put against your head and that'll be the end of you.

Here is a paper you must sign to say you are working on our side. Your signature will represent a lifelong commitment to our common cause, and you will promise to tell us anything and everything you know which may be of help to us. Now sign."

Jan reacted in anger.

"How can I be expected to help you and cooperate? In 1920 you tried to conquer us. In 1940 you took my mother, my sisters and me from our home in the middle of the night into exile, to face suffering, and possibly death. How can you expect me to join with you?"

The commissar had heard such statements a hundred times before. Now he wearily gave his response, which he knew he was almost certain to have to do when in front of these types. It was all so predictable.

"We were rescuing you from the Germans. Don't you understand? All you lot do is moan. Our own people live in exactly the same conditions as you have experienced here.

"Life is tough. Now sign the document that states you will be on our side wherever you are, wherever you may end up, and for as long as we hold you to your word. Sign that you are now one of us.

"The choice is yours."

Jan trembled with a combination of anger, humiliation and fear. He hesitated.

The clerk grew impatient, frustrated at the length of time this mundane task was taking because of the obstinate pride of this stupid young Pole. He pointed, firstly to the gun, then the bread.

"I'm not bloody joking."

Feeling broken, Jan signed.

"Thank you" said the clerk in a soothing voice, then gave Jan the bread.

Later that year, Jan remembered the incident and realised he would have to spend the rest of his life avoiding any possible contact with the Soviet secret police.

The bread didn't last long of course, and signing up to be a Soviet sleeper agent didn't grant Jan any privileges. Their situation was getting worse. Janina's health was declining further. She looked close to death. It appeared that her kidneys were failing. Hunger remained an everyday reality without any sign of it ending. Jan felt there was a real possibility that not only his mother, but all of the family would die in this village.

He wanted to take a risk for himself and for the rest of the family. He thought that if he set off without the others to find the Polish recruitment camp, believed now to be in the city of Kermine, then there would be more food available for the others. Yet he knew that he was the strongest of the four. He could earn more food as and when work was available. How would his sisters cope without him if food ran short again, and was only available to those who met stringent targets?

He spoke to his mother about it.

"Go. Go. Whatever happens to us happens. You must go." Janina ordered him. She said to him that the struggle for Poland must be put ahead of the fear of what might happen to her and her daughters.

So the next morning, taking advice on what road to take, Jan set off on his own to try to find Kermine and the Polish army. Late in his life, in an interview, he said, "I didn't expect to see any of them again".

It was 10th February 1942, two years to the day that they were deported from their home. The locals were angry at Jan's departure. A family had allowed their strongest worker to leave which meant that they, the villagers, were left with a sick mother, and two weak teenagers. The girls looked frail, more like children they were so under-developed. As a punishment the locals decided to stop giving the family any food at all.

In desperation Zosia and Danka would get up early in the morning and sneak into all the surrounding fields. There they dug up with bare hands anything they could find; the occasional carrot, potato or onion that had been missed during the harvest.

Sometimes they were caught and beaten for being thieves. They were insulted, called little vermin and a plague on the community.

With them in this village was a nine year old boy Jan Witkos. He was a friend of Danka's from their home village in Maczkowce. Jan's mother, Francisczka, was in a terrible condition, her stomach swollen due to severe malnutrition so Danka and her friend Jan went begging every day for food for their mothers.

For many years after the end of the war Danka thought that the little boy Jan must have died in the Soviet Union as she heard no news of him, but he did survive and was sent to an orphanage in South Africa until the end of the war. After Danka found out that Jan survived she tried to trace his parents but feared that they might not have got out of the Soviet Union during the war. In 2006 Jan's grandson Bernard got in touch with me by email from Dresden and confirmed that both his great grandparents – the little boy Jan's parents - died of starvation in Uzbekistan some time between 1941 and 1942, aged forty and thirty-eight respectively.

At every opportunity when she noticed little pieces of wool which had fallen from sheep or had got caught on a branch

Danka would collect it. She also pulled pieces from sheep when the locals weren't looking. Back in the hut each day she combed the wool with her thin fingers, took a stick and by turning it she started knitting the wool together. Eventually she managed to knit a jumper for herself from these scraps.

The locals then told Zosia that she could earn some food if she would work with others to dig up old roots in the now harvested cotton fields. She was given a heavy fork and daily targets to achieve, but her efforts were to no avail. She was simply too weak.

The locals gave her 150 grams of flour for her efforts on that first day of root digging. This was for all three remaining members of the family. On days when Danka was well enough to help they even managed to achieve the target and for this were given 500 grams.

When this work was complete Zosia was asked to dig canals for water but she knew that by now she was too weak to do it. Instead they began to sell any spare clothes they had, then with the money they bought some potatoes.

When these were eaten they returned to scratching in the fields for anything edible. Despite their exhaustion they walked as far as 4km to more distant fields. There was little left to forage and soon they completely ran out of roots to eat. So they resorted to ripping up grass and cooking it. Janina was slowly starving to death, lying all day in the corner of the mud hut.

Zosia recalled in an official report produced later that year how deeply she was affected by this desperate situation.

"I had to look after my mother and younger sister who were very weak. I was seventeen and I learned how difficult responsibility is. Being hungry and tired all the time I could see no way out of it. I thought I would go mad. Death from starvation was coming nearer and nearer."

After a few weeks there was no more grass to eat. Zosia and Danka went to a small market in a nearby village. There they sold a last pair of trousers that Jan had given them. They got 70 roubles for them; with this they bought 5kg of husks of wheat. Despite the fact that the husks were beginning to rot the girls went back to their hut happy that they had something to eat for the next few days. They had no fire or stove with which to cook the husks so they tried to make a form of pancake similar to what the locals made but they just crumbled. Still, it was food and every crumb was eaten.

Within a few days of eating the husks Janina's situation, rather than getting better, worsened. Something, possibly the rotten nature of the husks, or perhaps the amount of fibre in her emaciated body, caused her to have severe stomach pains.

The locals said they had no medicine to help Janina. Whether they were still punishing the Stepeks for allowing their son to leave the village, or simply because they had nothing to give which could help, we'll never know. A doctor lived seven kilometres away but the locals refused Zosia's pleas for the use of a farm horse to take Janina to the doctor. A horse was of great importance to the villagers' own everyday struggle to survive.

The husks had been eaten so they had no food left at all, and none likely to come their way from any local source.

Just in time, towards the end of February Polish officials provided help for the first time. They had been informed that Polish refugees were staying in this village. However, these officials had few resources to give as their efforts stretched thinly across a vast area in the south of the Soviet Union.

One of the Poles was given help by officials to travel to a small town. Zosia called it Saragaczu. He came back with 2kg of flour for the group. It had to suffice for the next month. They discovered that much of this food had been sent by Polish-Americans who were now becoming aware of the situation.

Over the next seven weeks Zosia walked four times with other refugees to Saragaczu to the Polish embassy's makeshift centre, to obtain further food for the family. Saragaczu was 30km away. She was the youngest in the group. Usually they received sacks of wheat or corn which Zosia had to carry all the way back by herself.

The group walked to the town and back in one journey, leaving at night and returning the following night as they had nowhere to sleep on the route or at Saragaczu itself.

Zosia remembers one particularly gruelling trip during this time. Having collected a twelve kilogramme sack of wheat, Zosia walked back the fifteen kilometres in very heavy rain. She had to trudge through miles of thick mud in her bare feet. After she got back to the village she lay down on the floor of the mud hut and was unable to stand up for the next three days.

Despite the extra food their health continued to decline. Most of their fellow Poles in the village were suffering similarly. A group discussed the perilous situation and agreed between them that Danka should leave with a group of women as she was the youngest and now very weak. This group would set off directly to a place called Jangi-Jul (or Jang-Jul as it was sometimes known). The officials had told them this was where the Polish officials had their centre. Everyone felt that Danka might be saved from starvation by this decision, so she left her sister and mother in the morning.

A week or so later, near the end of April 1942 Zosia and Janina left for the same destination. Zosia could only take what she could carry. These few items she carried ten kilometres to the train station because again the local people refused their pleas for the use of a horse. She sold everything else they had and with some of the little money she received, paid a local man to take Janina to the train station in a cart, as Janina still could not stand unaided.

Unknown to them at the same time Polish soldiers and officers were being sent by General Wladyslaw Anders to comb hundreds of villages and towns in vast areas, locate any children and take them to Tashkent. In all they gathered eighteen thousand children. General Anders knew that the parents or those adults left to fend for the children, would sacrifice themselves in order to feed the children. If the children were taken into care, Anders reasoned, the adults would be able to look after themselves better, freed from the duty of feeding children first.

Wrewsko and Karkin-Batash

April to May 1942

The group with whom Danka travelled walked much of the distance. Occasionally a passing train would stop for them when they signalled with their hands. An officer on board one train gave Danka some precious sliced bread. On another occasion as they walked through an Uzbeki farming village, a man came out of his house and gave pancakes to every child as they passed through. He, and other villagers who helped them throughout their long journey said to them,

"Pray for my son. He is at the front."

There seemed to be no one in the vast expanse of the Soviet Union who was not either grieving or suffering or both.

Danka arrived in a place named Kolchozy with the group of women. It was just outside Tashkent and had a makeshift refugee camp run by Polish officials. Despite this conditions remained very difficult, with shortage of food and a lack of medical staff and provisions with which to treat the wave of ill, malnourished men women and children who arrived each day.

Danka told an officer that she had a brother who had joined the army in this area. The officer told her that a newly-formed unit, made up of the Poles released from labour camps in the Soviet Union, had now embarked to Persia. So Danka thought that Jan, assuming he was still alive, would have already left the Soviet Union.

The officer investigated further and found that Jan had left all his earnings as a soldier for the rest of his family should they be found. Danka asked if he could send soldiers out with the money back to the village where Janina and Zosia remained begging for food to stay alive. Janina and Zosia did receive this desperately needed income and the good news that at least one member of the family may have already left the Soviet Union.

Danka's stay at Kolchozy was short-lived, and soon they were taken to the Polish Army regional headquarters at Jangi-Jul. There was still snow lying on the ground. Danka remembers that they were there before 3rd May because this date is Poland's National Day and she recalls being in Jangi-Jul marching despite their frailty and illnesses to a song with the words "One day we shall return to Poland".

She spent around three weeks at Jangi-Jul before the authorities decided to separate the children from the adults. It was realised that a wartime military headquarters was not equipped or suitable for sick and hungry children.

So in mid May the whole group of child refugees were transported to Wrewsko (also known as Vrevsko or

Wrewskaja), a town some forty miles south-west of Tashkent. A makeshift but large-scale orphanage had already been set up there for children separated from, or who had lost, their parents. It was run by the Polish army.

A week or two later Zosia arrived with Janina, via Tashkent. Zosia volunteered to help in the orphanage as she was one of the older girls there. She carried soup round the camp to feed the younger children.

Because of her grave physical state Janina was allowed to stay with her daughters, and despite shortages of food and resources her desperate condition started to improve a little.

However, their stay in Wrewsko was for only a few days as an order came from Polish army officials to move a group of the older girls to yet another camp. The officials had only now begun to see the enormous scale of the task in front of them. So many children needed help, so they decided to split the group into two. The younger ones would stay at Wrewsko, while the older girls, including Danka and Zosia would go to Karkin-Batash which was set up to deal with teenagers.

This meant they had to leave Janina behind. Zosia had been sharing her rationed food of bread and soup with her mother to strengthen her. At the camp Janina had met three women doctors who did all they could to help her, limited as they were by the difficult circumstances. Hundreds of others needed help. The doctors themselves were not well; and there was very limited resources of food or medicine.

Zosia went looking for the lady doctors and found them in a queue. She begged them to please care for her mother as she would have no one to look after her when the two girls were moved to Karkin-Batash. They agreed to do so. She found out later that the doctors agreed that at least one of the three would be there with Janina at any given time.

Zosia's mind was a bewildering series of emotions - despair, fear, hope and a constant sense of the dangers that were present for all of them, but especially for Janina.

Karkin-Batash proved to be an utter disaster. Arriving there sometime in June they found it to be a village of traditional Uzbeki mud houses and they discovered that 'Karkin-Batasz' means 'Valley of Death', something that proved to be prescient.

Danka described it as 'the worst place under the sun'. There were scorpions everywhere and the weather was unbearably hot. Very soon after they arrived many children became seriously unwell.

Zosia was still plagued with worry and guilt about leaving her mother. She lay on a mat, tired and weary, on the clay floor of the Uzbek mud hut which she shared with several other girls. She prayed each night asking God to keep Janina in His care.

Beside her was a girl of similar age. Tall, slender, with brown hair, beautiful eyes and a look of great intelligence. Her name was Janka. She was very self-controlled and made a great impression on Zosia who was struggling emotionally at the time.

Each day Zosia's highlight was receiving their small chunk of bread and a teaspoonful of sugar, plus a plate of pea soup. Zosia's disappeared in a flash, and she noticed her constant craving for food even when she was no longer hungry, so deep was the fear of a return to starvation.

Janka, in complete contrast, divided her portion of bread into two equal halves. One half she dried for use at a later date. Zosia asked her why she didn't just eat it all, as Zosia had done.

"I am keeping that half and drying it so it will last until I get the chance to give it to my mother. She is in an Uzbek village not too far away and is struggling with real hunger."

Shortly after this conversation Zosia fell ill with an unknown condition and was taken to another mud hut which served as a hospital. When she recovered well enough to leave the hospital and return to her own hut, Janka wasn't there. She had died of starvation.

Zosia's health didn't last much more than a few days. Awaiting a visit from Polish Bishop Gawlin Zosia started writhing with pain. She stayed to meet the bishop then was taken immediately to hospital again. She had dysentery.

Every morning soldiers had the heart-breaking duty of taking out those girls who had died through the night as a result of dysentery. There was simply no medicine with which to treat or ease the girls' conditions.

By this time of year the sun was baking hot at mid-day but there were so many girls ill with dysentery that many could not get into the mud hut hospital and had to lie outside. As there were no trees for shelter either the older girls chose to lie outside on a blanket, giving up their spaces in the hospital to the younger girls in order to protect them from the worst of the heat of the sun. No one had pillows on which to rest their head, inside or outside the hut, so they used their fists instead.

One sweltering hot day Zosia saw a little girl panting frantically for air. She seemed to be choking. Zosia pushed her way through the sprawled-out bodies of sick girls outside the hut. On reaching her, Zosia lifted the girl's head and soothed her so that she calmed down. She fell asleep resting her head on Zosia's shoulder. Within a few minutes she died, Zosia still cradling her in her arms.

Another day a girl, Halina, spread her blanket next to Zosia's outside the hospital. Her attitude was the opposite of Zosia's fear of death.

"So what, why should I be afraid? When it's time to die, you die."

Halina survived. We may never know how much attitude plays a part in survival of those who experience severe suffering, but many who do survive have a clear, strong perspective about life, and Halina was one of those.

Zosia recovered sufficiently to leave the hospital. Outside the camp area there was an oasis with a single tree, the only tree for miles. A Mrs. Koscialowska taught the girls maths there, which gave the girls something to focus on other than bread and the fear of falling prey to severe illness. Of course, there were no textbooks, paper, pens or pencils but the girls rose to the challenge and they learned.

At this time Danka fell gravely ill and for the first time it looked like she might not survive. She had been ill before during the time in the camp, and from the extreme hunger and thirst on the odyssey to the south. But she had not encountered the effects of disease such as she now experienced in the heat of Uzbekistan. The disease was never diagnosed, and somehow Danka recovered to some extent without the aid of medicines.

Martin Stepek

One day a group of adults arrived in the teenagers camp, in transit to another camp for adults. Danka saw her mother lying down amongst them. She rushed to see her, and for two days the three were reunited after which Janina left with the other adult refugees. While Danka and Zosia were at this camp money arrived from Jan who was now being paid as a member of the army. He had given the money to his superior officer and asked that it be given to his family wherever they may be. So Zosia bought some food for Janina and when her mother left, Zosia knew that Janina had some resources to help her survive. All three were deeply moved to learn that Jan was not only alive, but earning money, and still thinking of the wellbeing of his family.

Because of the scale of deaths in such a short period of time the army decided to evacuate many of the girls from the camp at Karkin-Batasz and move them a few miles south-west to Guzar. Zosia was given the option to stay or to go with Danka. She chose the latter. Apart from wanting to be with her sister Zosia was concerned that Danka would not survive another bout of the illness that had struck her, unless Zosia was there to attend to her.

In the month that Zosia and Danka stayed at Karkin-Batasz, ninety-two girls died out of a total of about three hundred who were there. Almost one in three. The mass graves are still there and Polish officials make visits to this day to commemorate the young Poles who died in this Valley of Death.

Guzar

Late May to Early August 1942

Guzar, further to the west, in present-day Turkmenistan, was to be their new camp. Conditions were much better. There was boiled water to drink, prepared in huge cauldrons and flavoured with tea. There was no milk or sugar but Zosia described it like "heavenly nectar". She drank and drank and drank it.

It reduced the stomach pains and internal bleeding which she had suffered from bouts of dysentery over many months. The pain and fears that come with dysentery was to haunt Zosia for many years, but at these moments in Guzar it felt like pure joy to be free of it if only for a short time.

Just outside the camp, groups of stray Polish children gathered begging for bread. No one knew where they had come from or how far they had travelled as there were no adults with them. They were part of the vast numbers not yet registered and cared for by the Polish officials and it took a long time to process them, check their health and bring them into the camp system, which was already bursting with stray and orphaned children. The officials were overwhelmed, emotionally as well as physically.

Zosia and many other girls put aside part of their daily bread ration to share with these unregistered waifs. Each day those registered also received a small cube of pressed dates. Zosia shaved off a tiny sliver of this for herself and gave the rest to the youngest child outside the camp. She wrote in her recollections that she hoped that God having noticed her sacrifice would return the favour by inducing someone to give food to her mother. She had no idea where Janina was now, nor how she was faring. This act of giving made her feel morally uplifted and she overcame the cravings for sweet things which she had had. This was made easier by the fact that she had not tasted anything sweet for so many months it felt overpowering to her.

Danka arrived separately in Guzar, but not long after Zosia. She was still seriously ill. They lived in tents but every morning it became unbearably warm. To help her Zosia took Danka every day to a place she had discovered just outside the camp. It was a cave in the rocks. There Zosia laid her down for the whole day because it was much cooler than in the tents or outside where there were no trees for shade.

They remained in Guzar for more than two months, safe but unwell and still very malnourished. Then in August 1942 they were informed that arrangements were being made to transport those well enough to the port of Krasnovodsk, (now Turkmenbasy in Turkmenistan) on the Caspian Sea. From there they would embark boats which would take them to Persia.

Persia. It sounded so exotic, so mysterious. But much more important, what it really sounded like was one single word – freedom! The excitement and anticipation was almost unbearable.

Soon the departure date was announced but disaster struck. Danka's illness suddenly worsened. She could not sit up or stand. She was unable to eat. Her mouth sealed up. In the camp there was no medicine available to treat her.

The Soviet officials liaising with the Polish officers had insisted that only those well enough to walk unaided would be allowed to leave the camp for the port and hence to Persia. The unwell would be left in the camp or sent to hospital under the Soviet system as Soviet citizens.

Zosia was filled with dread. The chances of someone already unwell surviving under the Soviet system were slim. She asked a nurse what she could do to help Danka recover well enough to walk to the trucks in the morning, and then onto the boat when they arrived at the docks. She explained that Danka was now very starved, had a soaring temperature, and was skeletal in appearance.

The nurse said "Try to get some grapes and feed the juice to your sister. It may reduce her temperature and give her enough energy to stand and walk."

Zosia knew there was a local market in a nearby village but the girls were not allowed to leave the camp. Moreover it was stated that on this particular day, the day before their departure, no one was to leave the camp, and the gates were shut and locked. This order was made to prevent girls leaving the camp as many had other family members outside the camp and were desperate to remain with them, even at the sacrifice of not leaving the Soviet Union.

The day before departure one girl managed to sneak out and drag her mother secretly into the camp. The authorities didn't notice so she and her mother managed to leave for the port among the confusion and sheer mass of people.

Zosia didn't have the same opportunity to help her mother and had no money with which to buy grapes in order to try to save Danka. She started to look round the camp wall and found a small gap where the wall had crumbled. It was just wide enough for her to wiggle through. So she went back to her hut and changed into civilian clothes, a skirt and a blouse in place of the army uniform they had all been given. She had no civilian shoes and didn't want to be recognised by locals as coming from the Polish forces, so she left barefoot. She covered her hair with a scarf as the local Muslim women did, and to hide her blonde hair which was so distinctive from the typical dark hair of the Uzbeks.

She took her ration of bread, and Danka's too, as Danka was unable to swallow. She then set off for the village. Bread was like gold in the region so she knew she would be able to sell it. All she cared about was obtaining money for as many grapes as she could buy.

She sold the bread to a man who ironically was of Polish heritage but whose family had lived in the region for more than two generations. He gave her a fair price so now she had the money she craved. Zosia bought as many grapes as she could and managed to return to the camp undetected. If she had been noticed it was likely that both she and Danka would not have been permitted to leave on the following day's departure.

Back in the hut where Danka lay, Zosia cut each grape in half and carefully squeezed its juice onto a teaspoon. Each drop seemed so precious. She poured it very slowly and carefully into her sister's barely opened mouth while holding the back of her head with her other hand. This she did until all the grapes were gone. Hoping for a miracle she prayed to God to save Danka then left her for her own bed in another part of the camp.

With dawn came the morning of the momentous departure for the docks, from which - though few could scarcely believe it would happen - they would sail at last out of their captivity to something called freedom. Freedom of a sort, any sort. It had become a mantra, an abstract yearning in the heads of all those in the camp. Faced with the alternative of being left behind to live out their lives in the Soviet Union, everyone was in a state of desperate hope.

No one was allowed to leave their bedsides until everything was organised. The instructions came: at eight o'clock in the morning they had to go to the transport and not make a fuss over family or friends. They had to do so in silence, in a disciplined military way, then board the trucks which would take them to a train station. There they were to immediately board the train.

When she arrived at the train station Zosia climbed onto the train still unaware whether Danka had recovered sufficiently to get on one of the trucks. She had looked around her at all the others walking to the trucks. She had looked as much as she could at those boarding. She had looked as they got off the trucks and marched to the trains. No sight of Danka anywhere. She had no idea if her sister was sitting somewhere on the train or had been left to die in the camp.

As the train set off Zosia was stiff as a board with fear that Danka had been left behind. She was in floods of tears. Then she saw her walking towards her, or rather stumbling in a slow, sickly dazed way.

"I'm hungry. Give me something to eat."

Zosia asked her if she hadn't been given any rations of food, as Zosia and everyone else seemed to have. Danka took out her food, achingly, slowly like an infirm old woman.

"I want you to feed me." she said.

She didn't have the strength or mental control to do it herself so Zosia fed her sister water and bread like a mother to a sick infant.

Danka told Zosia some months later that she had been barely able to walk at the time of evacuation but friends discretely held her up when she stumbled or collapsed until she managed to get on the train.

Later they found out what had happened to many of the other families from their home village of Maczkowce, who had left Charytonowo labour camp earlier than the Stepek family did. Their journey led them to Alma-Ata, now Almaty, in eastern Kazakhstan, near the Chinese border. From there they were taken in a similar route to Zosia and Danka, and told that they would the board boats to Persia at Krasnovodsk. However many were told on arrival at the port that only able-bodied men were permitted to board. No women. No children. Thus many men left to join the armed forces whilst the women and children were forced to return to Alma-Ata. Only in 1956 were these families permitted to leave and return to new lives in communist Poland. One man named Polawski, the Stepek's nearest neighbour in

Maczkowce, and Danka's godfather, killed himself in post-war Poland after failing to discover his family. He thought they were dead but unknown to him they were still in Alma-Ata.

Jan in the Polish Army February to August 1942

Jan had walked for two full days barefoot, surviving on the generosity of the local Uzbek people as he wandered through their villages. Now he found himself at a Polish army recruitment and training camp at Choc-Pak (alternatively spelled Chokpak or Shoqpaq). Today it has a population of 1834 people spread over a five-mile radius. In 1942 it was used as a holding place for the Poles. It is in the far south of Kazakhstan, near the border with Kyrgyzstan, and only three hundred miles from the Chinese border. The family had not only travelled a huge distance to the south but also unknowingly far to the east. Jan was amazed that he was so close to China and realised that the rest of his family were even further east by some fifty to eighty miles. He bitterly reflected that they had wandered aimlessly, and at what cost?

Jan was told that the distant mountains to the south were in Afghanistan, some six hundred miles away, and Choc-Pak itself lies at an altitude of a thousand meters so in February it rapidly became cold at night.

Jan's official army records show that he was enlisted on arrival on the 10th of February 1942 into the newly formed Polish 8th Infantry Division. These are the first official records we have of any of the deported members of the family since they left the camp five months earlier.

There was no food available for him when he arrived at the army camp, but once the enlisted soldiers had finished eating he was allowed to have any leftovers. He was literally starving. The camp had no plates or cutlery so he poured leftover soup into a hat that he had stolen and ate it from that.

The next day he volunteered to work in the kitchen, saying he had experience as a chef. He wanted to be as close to the source of food as possible. Part of this work entailed Jan going to the well several times a day to fill large pots with water for cooking.

On one occasion, very early in the morning, having filled the pot, he carried the now heavy load back towards the kitchen tent but slipped on the icy ground and fell backwards spilling the entire contents of the pot onto himself. Thinking nothing of this Jan walked back towards the well to refill the pot but as he stepped he felt his movements increasingly restricted. Then he started to hear cracking sounds. The water which had spilled onto him had soaked into his clothing and onto his skin. It was freezing as he walked. He managed to fill the pot and return it to the kitchen but by the time he got there the clothes on the front of his body were enclosed in sheets of thick ice and had to be broken with a hammer by one of his colleagues before he could strip off his frozen and bitterly cold clothes.

Another time during his first few days in the camp, Jan was ordered to take a meal to one of the officers. The officer was friendly and offered him some vodka. He declined but the officer insisted. However, Jan was so malnourished and underweight that he was completely drunk by the time he walked the short distance back to the army kitchens. There he fell into one of the huge kitchen kettle drums used for cooking meals and slept the night there.

A week or so later in early March 1942, while standing on parade, he collapsed. He was diagnosed with typhus, taken to another tent attached to the camp and placed in a makeshift bed. Around him were scores of other men. They were all in a desperate state; feverishly hot then chilled to the marrow, malnourished with blinding headaches, weaker and weaker by the day.

Each morning those who died during the night were taken out for burial. Jan saw hundreds die in that tent in the months that he battled the disease. He had lost all hope of survival and fully expected to die. He couldn't hold down food and had no appetite. He started a macabre daily ritual. When he awoke each morning he reached down to check how thin his legs were by trying to encircle them with his hand. Eventually he grew so thin that he could completely encircle his thighs between the thumb and middle finger of each hand.

In late March and April the Polish troops started to leave their base camps and head to the port of Krasnovodsk on the shores of the Caspian Sea where they would embark Soviet boats and ships which would take them out of the Soviet

Union to Persia. The bulk of these forces, comprising over seventy thousand men previously labouring in the Gulag, had initially assembled at Buzuluk in southern Russia, close to the border with Kazakhstan, between Orenburg and Samara. The leadership of this unique rescue campaign, combining recovery through medical treatment and mass transportation was the task of General Wladyslaw Anders, who had himself been captured early in the war and suffered torture in Moscow. Now he was officially an ally of the Soviet Union, and his troops were thereafter called Anders' Army.

However, those suffering from typhus were deemed too ill to leave, so they missed this first opportunity to get out of the country in which they had, by now, felt imprisoned for over two years. Most were facing a desperate struggle to survive so were barely aware of the first evacuations. A team of doctors and nurses had stayed behind to look after them, but despite their efforts, thousands more died from typhus without tasting the freedom which awaited them on the other side of the Caspian Sea.

Jan survived and recovered sufficiently to continue his army work in the kitchens and elsewhere. It was now a much depleted camp so there was not a lot to do. As spring moved towards summer Jan's health improved. Food was still insufficient to make up for the lost years of malnutrition, so his physical growth as a late teenager was almost completely stunted. He was now nineteen. A sense of how precious life is

777777777777777

grew in his mind, aided considerably by the greater sense of security his position in the army gave him, and by the first experience of real consistent warmth in the hot but not oppressive Kazakh sun in those days.

Finally, in late July, preparations were made so that early the next month all remaining Polish troops not directly responsible for the evacuation of the tens of thousands of Polish civilians who remained in the Soviet Union, were to be transported to Persia. They were to pack up and leave the following week, the first week of August.

Jan was overjoyed but it didn't last. He fell seriously ill with dysentery. His already weakened body was in no shape to combat the illness, and he could barely stand. So on the day of departure, he was carried to a truck for the long, painful trip to the sea.

At the port Jan began to feel better and was able to walk with the help of a friend onto the ship at Krasnovodsk. It was a freighter called the Baku.

He lay down on the first deck he came to, alongside hundreds of other sick soldiers. The smell of excrement from these dysentery-struck young men was overpowering as it flowed onto the deck. Jan managed to pull himself up and found a space away from the dysentery-suffering soldiers. He sat upright for the whole journey, still covered in the foul-smelling human excrement. Yet on the journey, which lasted around 30 hours, Jan felt his health returning. The dysentery, if not its smell, had left him.

Then the day itself arrived. A day which Jan often thought would never happen, despite his early youthful bravado about leaving the labour camp and getting out of the Soviet Union. So much had happened to him in the intervening two and a half years that survival was all that mattered to him. Freedom, his homeland, even his family, existed only as fragments buried deep in the dark caverns of his mind.

Excitement grew. People started a babble of conversation, and though he couldn't make out what they were saying he knew they were off the coast of Persia. Free! They didn't know it then but what they saw was the port of Pahlevi (now called Bandar Anzali). Jan got up and looked. On the sandy beach he could see miles of tents and tarpaulins held up by bamboo branches, and a sea filled with people. They were lying, sitting, standing in the water, absorbing its miraculous healing qualities as the waves washed over them. Jan found out later that they were all Poles, earlier arrivals off the refugee boats.

Jan was helped down off the ship and immediately allocated to a hospital tent. Despite feeling that his health was restored, the medical staff took one look at him and decided otherwise. They made it clear to him that he was nowhere near well enough to rejoin the troops who were camped towards the back of the shore.

Martin Stepek

The Final Journey of Liberation

August 1942

The train arrived at the port of Krasnovodsk in Turkmenistan and immediately everyone was lined up to board the ship. They had travelled a total distance of over eight hundred miles west under Polish supervision since they had arrived in Uzbekistan some six months earlier.

Zosia managed to help Danka aboard where they stood crammed like sardines in one of the upper decks as there was no space for them to sit or lie down.

Zosia looked down and saw hundreds upon hundreds of other girls on the lower deck, jammed one against the other, but lying down. Zosia left to find the Russian in charge of the evacuation and explained that her sister was very sick and asked him if he could help find Danka a space so she could lie down on the deck. He agreed but as there was hardly any space, it would have to be on an upper deck. Somehow Zosia managed to get Danka up the narrow metal steps to the upper deck where there was a tiny space for Danka to lie down. Zosia couldn't remember whether Danka managed to walk to the upper deck or had to be helped. However, when they got to the allocated space Zosia laid her down carefully. She had obtained a small pillow and some water bought with the money from the bread she had sold the day before they left.

This proved to be life-saving as there was no drinking water on the ship. People died of dehydration on the journey but Zosia managed to eke out the small amount of water she had so that it lasted them the whole journey. She had to carefully put water into Danka's mouth as Danka couldn't do it herself. And so, the two sisters survived like this, where many others succumbed on the ship, dying just when rescue, freedom, and hope were almost in their grasp.

Finally after two days and nights in dreadful conditions the ship arrived at Pahlevi on the southern edge of the Caspian Sea. The sisters were able to see the land as they got closer to it. This was Persia.

But Zosia's mind was fretful. She cried, thinking "My God, how am I going to get Danka down amongst all these people? Please God help her."

Waiting desperately in their upper deck Zosia watched the mass of unwashed, skeletal humanity disembark onto the shoreline. Then a Polish soldier appeared beside them. He said nothing at all, just picked up Danka, cradled her like a baby, and took her down stair after stair, then off the ship to the shores of Pahlevi. Zosia followed in his footsteps and said it felt like arriving in Heaven, a genuine feeling like a religious redemption.

It was part of a much larger long-term plan which had begun several months earlier in Moscow. After tense negotiations the Polish Prime Minister and head of the armed forces, General Wladyslaw Sikorski met with Josef Stalin and agreed an evacuation of those Poles taken to the Soviet Union in 1940 and later.

The operation was code-named Scalene by the British and originated in the Soviet desire to have Poles recruited and trained for the defence of the Soviet Union against the invading German forces. For Sikorski however it was about releasing and training Poles for the eventual liberation of Poland, and the evacuation of sick and starving men, women and children from Soviet soil to a safer country.

In order to speed up the slow, frustrating pace of progress in the recruitment, training and evacuation of the Poles in Russia, an Anglo-Polish team departed for Pahlevi in Mid-February to make preparations for receiving the evacuees and Polish troops from the Soviet Union. In March Stalin personally laid out the land and sea route by which the Poles would cross the Caspian Sea via Krasnovodsk.

The order for commencing the evacuations was made on 23rd March 1942 and the first ship full of Poles left the following day from Krasnovodsk, arriving in Pahlevi a day later. On board were almost fourteen hundred recently recruited members of the Polish armed forces.

Several other evacuations by boat were to follow. In the first month alone seventy-seven thousand soldiers and thirty thousand civilians, including fifteen thousand children left Krasnovodsk.

The Journey across the Caspian was a distance of around four hundred and eighty kilometres (three hundred miles). The fastest of any of the journeys lasted twenty-seven hours, on a steam tanker which had the good fortune of mild weather and no engine or mechanical problems en route.

Depending on the size of the boat being used, the final stage of the journey was sometimes accomplished using smaller boats to take the Polish civilians or soldiers right to the shore, with the main vessel anchored further out at sea, as some of the boats were too large for the narrow port at Pahlevi. This necessitated a much slower process. The longest disembarking took twelve hours, unloading some five thousand, four hundred refugees. The average time it took to get from ship to shore was four to five hours. It was a case of so near yet still so far for the desperately hungry and thirsty people who could see the haven that was Persia awaiting them.

Sadly it was much worse for some. Several smaller ships and boats bringing evacuees across were sunk in stormy weather, with all on board drowned, therefore, although their journey was awful, Zosia and Danka were in fact fortunate on this, the final leg of their journey out of the Soviet Union.

Pahlevi August 1942

On arrival in Pahlevi the refugees were met by British and Polish Red Cross medical teams who, with the aid of soldiers, helped the sickest off the boat. Everyone who disembarked was kept in the hospital tents for a minimum of three weeks, quarantined in order to prevent epidemics in Persia. So many of the people on board had major tropical diseases that the risk to their new host country was very real.

After a time left lying on the shore with the waves gently washing over and soothing her, Danka was taken to a tent for those in need of intensive care. There the medical teams gave the weakest and sickest specially selected food as very weak digestive systems can react violently to receiving ordinary foods or too much food which may result in the death of those with such extreme conditions. Tragically this was only discovered by the medical teams when witnessing the deaths of many hundreds of earlier evacuees.

While Danka was in this special unit Zosia had managed to walk off the ship unaided. However she was in a very poor condition, her body emaciated, every rib visible, and her legs were like sticks. Her skin was covered in ulcers. Despite this she acted the part of the soldier she now was, taking part in marches which were arranged to boost morale. After one such march an Indian nurse asked her in sign language how Zosia's arms could be so thin. Zosia raised her arms and shoulders.

"How on Earth could I start to explain?" she told me.

Zosia visited Danka every day and spent as much time with her as possible. Every day she also asked officials about recent and new arrivals, names, dates. She was looking for news of Janina, and Jan too as she had had no news of him for several months.

The Polish refugee and hospital camp at Pahlevi was huge, stretching three miles along the sandy beach, a vast array of banana leaf canopy roofs held up by bamboo sticks. This was to shield the suffering from sunstroke in the Persian summer heat.

These makeshift hospital tents were stretched out along the full length of the camp, in one long row nearest to the sea. Behind this were two rows of tents which housed the army and Red Cross.

Zosia made her way systematically through the hospital areas searching for her mother. They were full of people of all ages and sizes, all sick, all weak.

One day an officer told her that her mother had arrived on a ship the previous night and was in the civilian camp, which was separate from but adjacent to the army camp. Zosia ran from the one camp to the other and searched frantically through each section, looking, double-checking, but she was nowhere to be found.

Then she saw her.

And Janina saw her daughter.

The mother uttered the daughter's name, "Zosia", and fainted at the shock of seeing Zosia, dressed in uniform, washed and seemingly in reasonable health. It was more than she could have dreamed of.

A few weeks' later Zosia found Jan.

She told me,

"One day I remember finding your father. He was lying on the ground in a tent, there in Pahlevi. He looked like a small boy, all shrivelled. I still remember to this day looking at him. I couldn't speak. I was overcome with emotion. He was so starved, so shrunken. I was completely choked."

My father verified this description of the severe state he was in. He was a month short of his twentieth birthday. His habit of measuring his thigh's thickness became his way of judging whether he was getting closer to death or heading in a healthier direction.

Jan had partially recovered from dysentery in the days leading up to his departure from the Soviet Union but was still physically spent. According to his military records he was officially re-enlisted into the army on the 15th August, as being in "service with the Polish Land Forces under British Command". This was probably his date of arrival in Pahlevi.

Danka too remained close to death. She was weighed in the hospital tent in Pahlevi, wearing an adult Polish army uniform. She weighed only twenty-five kilogrammes, (three stone and thirteen pounds in imperial terms). She was fifteen years old. She was to spend six weeks in the hospital area of Pahlevi before she was deemed well enough to move to the civilian camp.

Most of those in hospital suffered from night-blindness due to malnutrition. Fortunately Danka was spared this but she remembers the tragi-comedy played out every night in the tents. Hundreds of those who were ill suffered terribly from dysentery, which required them to go to the toilet frequently and with great urgency. This included going in the middle of the night. There was minimal lighting in the hastily put-together camp so the poor night-blind sufferers stumbled over other patients to find their way to holes dug in the sand which served as toilets. Some would fall in, other would miss the hole completely as they emptied their bowels. Still others wouldn't manage to get out of the tent before their bowels opened. For those who did manage to reach the toilets and relieve themselves properly, the steps back to their tent was chaotic. They couldn't see so tried to guess their direction, feeling their way and hoping they had counted the right numbers of tents to get back to their own one. Many ended up lying across other patients, in the wrong tent, and facing in the wrong direction.

Constantly through the night there were whispered shouts of "Is this Tent Number Three?", "Danka, are you there?" or "Is this my bed?"

Danka eventually became well enough to be allowed a degree of free movement within the confines of the camp. The first thing she did was try to visit her mother, only to be told that she had been taken to a hospital in Teheran because of how unwell she was.

She then visited Jan, seeing him for the first time in six months. Like Zosia she was shocked by his shrunken, skeletal appearance. Now he lay ill on a mat beside a young Jewish man. All three of them would share cooked fish brought by the nurses who firstly had to establish that each patient was now well enough to take such a rich form of food.

One day, feeling stronger than usual Jan and his friend left the tent without permission and went to a local market. They had been allowed to venture into the warm sea and gently strengthen their arms by swimming for a few minutes. They did this as normal before sneaking out of the camp zone. They stole two bottles of wine from a trader's stall, and bartered one of the bottles for kebab meat, which they had never tasted before. It was the finest most succulent flavour Jan could imagine. Lying with the first taste of wine he had experienced since being taken from Poland more than two years earlier, Jan felt he was on the point of regaining normal healthy life.

Within an hour though his stomach started cramping and it rapidly grew worse. They made it back to the camp, where Jan's situation was by then deemed so serious he was taken directly to a hospital in Teheran. His dysentery had returned, and in his weak state, was considered unlikely to survive. He thought in despair, referring to his thievery of the bottles of wine "I never knew God could punish so quickly."

The following morning Danka came to visit him to be told that he too was now transferred to Teheran. She in turn told Zosia that the four members of the family were now in two different places, but with Janina and Jan transported on different dates and with different illnesses, it was unlikely that the mother and her son would ever have been aware of each other's location.

Whilst in Pahlevi Zosia took a school examination. She qualified for the upper form of the newly formed grammar school despite having missed three years of education. She was now seventeen. As part of the examination the girls had to write an essay on "Thoughts and Dreams After Crossing the Soviet Border."

She was now a schoolgirl soldier having travelled a total of six thousand miles to get to a place of freedom, and it had taken them ten months to do so.

Ironically Persia was itself a country under occupation, invaded by both British and Soviet forces in order to prevent the Persian government from providing technology and trade to Germany, with whom they had had good relations prior to the onset of the war.

Danka was finally deemed well enough to leave Pahlevi and be transferred to Teheran with Zosia. The exact date is unknown but probably early October 1942, a month or so after Janina's then Jan's departures.

"They were beautiful people." said Danka referring to the Persian people. "In Pahlevi they were always bringing food. Food and more food to us. I don't think they had ever seen people in as bad a state as we were."

A British Army report was published about the second evacuation of Poles from the USSR to Pahlevi in that August of 1942, the month during which all four of the Stepeks arrived in Persia. One section concerned those child and teenage refugees placed in a special hospital tent because of the severity of their ill-health. This would have included all three of the Stepek children. A single sentence from the report records their plight and the speed of their initial recovery: "Their average stay in the camp was seven and a half days, and their average increase in weight during this period was twenty-one pounds and one ounce."

Teheran

October 1942 to March 1943

I am a member of an online research group made up of descendants of the deportees from Poland to the Soviet Union. One day the group received a message from the son of a British doctor who had treated the Poles when they arrived in Teheran. Unfortunately I didn't note his name but he shared with the group a short extract from his father's diary at that time. It dates from April 1942, and thus was some six months before the Stepeks arrived, but it is one of very few written contemporary impressions of the situation.

"A hundred cases of typhus for me to examine and treat. I have been at it all day. Half of them were lying on the floor with their kits beside them. I found lice on four patients even though disinfestation had already been done at Pahlevi."

The trip from Pahlevi to Teheran was by truck, a journey of two hundred and twenty miles. Danka was still ill when she arrived so was taken straight to one of the hospitals set up to treat the Poles in the capital. Unlike in Pahlevi all of these hospitals were in buildings.

Although still unwell, after a few weeks Danka was told she would be discharged from the hospital and was allocated to Polish Refugee Camp Number 1 which was a camp specialising in helping sick children on their release from acute illness hospitals. In total there were four camps for Polish refugees in the city.

Zosia was in Polish Refugee Camp Number 2. It was now around 20th October. Zosia recalled feeling stronger and sensed that she was growing again due to the plentiful supply of healthy food, after years of stunted growth due to malnutrition. One day she had the luxury of going into a bath and saw that her legs resembled a zebra's, alternating white and dark stripes. She was stretching in height so fast that new light-coloured skin was developing in between sections of her deeply tanned older skin.

Earlier Danka was told to register at Camp Number 1 so joined the queue in order to enrol. There she was met and greeted by her uncle, Henryk Ciupka, Janina's eldest brother. He was a senior officer in the army. His daughter Henryka was also in Teheran, a captain at the age of twenty-seven. Now Danka had extended family to help and support her.

Henryk told Danka that Janina was in a hospital camp in another part of the capital. Danka, still not strong enough to go, passed on a message to Zosia and Zosia immediately went there. Janina was lying down on a bed. She took one look at Zosia then slipped into sleep or unconsciousness.

Danka managed to visit her the following day, and her mother could barely speak to her, she was so frail.

Zosia visited her mother again on 24th October, and Janina was able to speak with her for a few minutes. She told her that she had been taken to Teheran some days before the daughters arrived and that there was nothing special provided for her despite her severe illness and weakness. There was probably little the medical team could do for her.

Janina asked Zosia to bring her some water, boiled so that it would be free of any germs but there was no fire burning nearby with which to heat the water so Zosia couldn't give her the water she asked for. Zosia returned to the camp where she was staying. She requested and was granted a temporary transfer from the military school camp at which she had been enrolled, to the main civilian camp which was nearer to where Janina was hospitalised.

On the morning of 25th October Danka tried again to visit Janina but there were too many people already queued up to get onto the army trucks that took people from that camp to other camps and to hospitals. So she had to wait two or three hours for the next available trucks. Finally, she got a lift and arrived at the hospital.

Janina's bed was empty.

A woman, probably a nurse, looked at Danka with a pained expression.

"Your mother died this morning. She is already in a coffin. Would you like to go with her to the cemetery?"

She was led outside. On the back of a flat-bed truck were five coffins. One of them contained Janina's body but no one knew which one. Danka was told to sit with others who were already sitting on top of the coffins. It was just about to leave for the cemetery. The others on the truck were kind and asked Danka who she was, and other questions but Danka was in a daze and couldn't remember any answers to the questions, nor even her own name. She was desolate.

They arrived at the cemetery in Doulab, a suburb in the east of the city. The coffins were unloaded and gently lowered into a wide, deep pit, one alongside the next. There were no labourers there at the time to fill the graves with soil so the five coffins lay exposed to the open air.

After the burial Danka declined to get back on the truck to return to the camp. She stayed there at the cemetery for some time in a numbed state, staring at the five coffins in the pit, not knowing which one contained her mother's body.

Eventually she left the cemetery and started running wherever her feet took her, and by sheer luck ran in the right direction, not stopping until she reached the camp.

As Danka was watching her mother's coffin being lowered into the mass grave Zosia had arrived at the hospital to be told that Janina had died and had been taken away to be buried.

The two sisters were still not in the same camp so each spent hours alone with their numbing grief, and visited Janina's grave in Doulab every day.

I asked Danka about this pivotal experience in her life.

"I knew well that mother would not survive. There was no hope. She was destroyed by what they did to her in Poland. She was a very gentle person."

If fate had been kinder, she might have survived and recovered. I am sad that she never had the chance to know her eighteen grandchildren of which I am one. The youngest of us was born in 1966, and Janina was born in 1902 so she could have known us all. She could never have imagined, as her life ebbed away in the autumn air of Persia, that one day her children's children would prosper in Scotland, England, Portugal, Holland, France, Poland and Canada. Many would visit a free Poland, enter the home her husband was born in, some even work or deliver talks in Warsaw.

There was no sign of Jan. Records showed that he had arrived in the capital, enrolled in a camp, but he was no longer there and no one could provide further details. The family were able to confirm that he was not on the meticulously-kept, rapidly growing list of those who had died and been buried in the city. Henryk and his daughter Henryka checked all official documents daily, and regularly called in to all the military and civilian camps, and the various hospitals.

"Is there a Jan Stepek here?"

Always the same answer. It was a mystery.

Danka meanwhile was moved from Camp Number 1 to a barracks given over to the Polish government as the base for a nearby school for Polish orphans. She was able to restart her school education, at primary school level despite being fifteen. She had missed three years of education in the Soviet Union. The school was in a separate barracks from where they slept, situated just outside of Teheran in an area populated by holiday homes for the more well-off city dwellers.

Danka's primary school work finished in mid-November 1942 and she was free thereafter to roam the various Polish camps. Just before Christmas, their cousin Henryka discovered where Jan was. He had been taken to a small specialist hospital set up in a disused factory. It was called W Hospital and was overseen by American medics, hence the reason why Jan seemed to slip out of the Polish records. It is likely that his condition had been so grave that the Americans urgently took him in as an emergency case and in the rush the normal paperwork and protocols had been forgotten.

Henryka visited him. She had to break the news of his mother's death, but also that his two sisters were still alive.

My father told me that he felt no emotion when he heard the news of his mother's death. He thought it only a matter of time before he died too, so from that perspective it hardly mattered. He had been so close to death for almost the whole of 1942, with only the briefest respite in August, that he had no energy left to create a glimmer of hope or optimism.

Danka and Zosia went to visit him with their Uncle Henryk. Since they last saw him he had turned twenty years old. No one had been with him on his birthday except the doctors and nurses in the W Hospital. No one knew it was his birthday, least of all Jan himself. If he had known, he wouldn't have cared except to admit the irony of dying just as you reach manhood. And had he not been forced to become a man so many years ago?

It was the first time that the three siblings had been together since Jan had left the family to join the Polish army in early February. In that time the effects of typhus, two bouts of dysentery, and now, the girls learned, malaria, had all taken their toll. Desperately weak and malnourished the doctors and nurses still tended him but told the girls they did not expect him to survive. They had moved him to the bed nearest the morgue.

Danka through much of this time wore only a ragged nightdress day and night, awake and asleep. She had no spare clothes and had spent two full months wearing only that nightdress, and only had footwear because her aunt Wanda, Henryk's wife, managed to find her an extra pair of old shoes that had belonged to Danka's cousin, Dobrusia, who was the same age.

Despite his frailness Jan was able to think clearly at times. He still received money from his pay in the army. He gave it to Wanda when she visited one day and asked her to buy material to make a new dress for Danka.

Around New Year Danka suffered badly from scurvy and was hospitalised again. When Henryk came to visit her he brought some tomatoes to help speed up the healing. Danka hadn't seen a tomato since they had left Poland. She added a little salt to it and bit into the ripe fruit. The pain was unbearable as the combination of salt and acidic juice from the tomato penetrated the raw wounds inside her mouth. However by the next day the scurvy was already fading and the wounds healing over.

Ironically given how ill he was, it was Jan who was first of the three siblings to leave Persia. Having spent a total of six months in hospital in Teheran, his body started to rebuild a little strength day by day in early 1943. Although he later described that period in Teheran as an eternity in hell, he now regained the determination to not only survive but recover.

The staff who nursed and treated him were primarily Indian and Pakistani. It was due to their skill and tireless efforts that he survived, and as a little extra gift they taught him his first three words of English. Ravaged by another bout of dysentery whilst suffering from malaria, he learned these vital - and urgent – words:

"Mister, bedpan please!"

By late January 1943, he had sufficiently recovered to be able to leave the hospital and prepare to re-join his army unit, which was now engaged in training exercises in Basra, Iraq, a journey of over five hundred miles by truck.

Less than two months later in Teheran Polish officials asked for young people to join an army youth group called the Young Volunteers. To qualify you had to be sixteen and pass a medical examination. Danka and Zosia went together even though Danka was still only fifteen. Zosia told Danka to go first reasoning that if they accepted Danka, they would accept Zosia so as to remain with Danka and care for her as she was still very unwell.

Danka was frightened that the doctor would ask her date of birth; she was not only underage but still looked even younger because her body was still frail and weak so Danka told Zosia to go first.

They asked Zosia her date of birth and weighed her, both things Danka feared when it came her turn. Zosia was accepted but when Danka went in the doctor immediately said "Oh no, under age, under weight."

The doctor added her name to a list of orphans to be sent to India for the rest of the war as part of a plan to move all the remaining civilians out of Persia. The bulk of Polish civilians were to go to British-occupied Palestine. Others were to be sent to three settlements in Africa. Uncle Henrik's wife Wanda and their youngest daughter, Dobrusia were told they were being sent to Rhodesia. Now Danka was to be sent to India.

When the doctor informed Danka he saw her distraught expression and said "Do you have any family here?"

"My sister Zosia. You have just accepted her for the Young Volunteers. Also I have my Uncle Henryk Ciupka and his daughter Henryka. They are officers in the army. Please don't send me to India by myself."

The doctor scored out Danka's name from the list of those to go to India. She then put Danka's name on the list for those accepted as Young Volunteers, and changed her date of birth on the form by one year. Decades later in The Polish Institute and Sikorski Museum in South Kensington, London, Zosia saw the original document including the list with

Danka's name on it and the date of birth changed by one year exactly.

When Danka came out from her medical examination, she threw her arms around Zosia's neck and cried.

"Don't ever leave me. I want you to stay with me."

It was decided that the Young Volunteers were to go to Palestine. They were taken from their barracks in April 1943 and spent the next three months in quarantine not far from Teheran. It was a desert region, dazzled with beauty. Springtime had brought a full carpet of different coloured flowers. They witnessed dramatic desert storms, from the safety of their tents. As one of the older girls Zosia accompanied the girls and oversaw routine matters. She had turned eighteen and taken the military oath. She was now once more a soldier in the Polish Army.

In July 1943 the two sisters finally left Persia, leaving their mother. None of the three Stepek siblings were ever to return to visit her grave.

Several thousand Poles who had somehow survived the odyssey from their places of captivity in the Soviet Union to this land of freedom had fallen just at their moment of freedom. Their graves would be tended by generations of Poles and Iranians in the decades that followed.

Danka and Zosia had spent eleven months in this, their first haven of peace and care since war had broken out almost four years earlier. Now they were headed for Rehovets in Palestine, another epic journey of over one thousand miles, this time in military trucks as part of a massive convoy transporting survivors of the dreadful Siberian experience.

Palestine and Egypt

July 1943 to 1947

Zosia and Danka were among five thousand Polish orphans and other Polish civilians sent to Palestine in 1943. An additional twenty-eight thousand Poles who found themselves in Teheran after their Soviet ordeal were sent that year to a bewildering array of destinations: Lebanon, India, Uganda, Kenya, Tanganyika, South Africa, Southern and Northern Rhodesia, and as far afield as Mexico and New Zealand. A few hundred chose to stay in Persia, where their children and grandchildren still live as Polish Iranians, mostly in and around Teheran.

Polish institutes were established in Palestine, around Rehovets, Nazareth and Qastina: schools, scout and guide groups, a Women's Auxiliary Service, an Officers' Legion, and military training centres. New educational materials were written and printed for the schools to enable all those whose school education had been interrupted by the deportations to restart formal education and catch up the school years they had lost. It was also designed to normalise the lives of people who had known great alienation and suffering for over three years.

Danka, just turned sixteen, had already resumed her school education in Teheran and was determined to make up the lost years by striving to learn all that she could in the peaceful surroundings of Palestine.

She and Zosia were placed in an orphans' barracks in Rehovets, midway between Jerusalem and Tel Aviv. The Polish school was nearby. The sisters felt that Palestine was like Paradise. Everywhere was green. Fruit grew in abundance. All along the seashore were orange groves, so many that much of the fruit rotted because the war had interrupted the region's export markets. Arab children went into the Polish settlements selling bags of fruit for a few pennies.

Not long after they had settled in Rehovets the two girls were transferred to another Polish base in Qastina, now called Be'er Tuvia. This was a little south of Tel Aviv, and west of Jerusalem, not far from the sea. It was there that Danka passed the final year of her primary school education in 1943 at the age of fifteen.

Within days of their arrival in Qastina, General Sikorski, the President and Head of Armed Forces of Poland came to Palestine and visited the children at the orphans' school camp. Danka felt no warmth towards him. On the other hand, she felt deep affection and gratitude towards General Anders who frequently visited the Polish girls and boys in the region. He spoke to them as "my children" and drew up plans for a new future for this coming generation in post-war Poland.

It was one of the last formal actions by General Sikorski. A few days later the plane he was on crashed on take-off from Gibraltar. Poland had lost its wartime leader and it proved to be a political and military catastrophe for Poland.

Later that year came the most important and emotional experience of Zosia and Danka's Palestinian years. A group of the sisters' girl friends from the orphan camp had a day off and travelled to the port of Haifa. There they discovered to their delight that a Polish ship was docked at the harbour and scores of young Polish sailors, looking splendid in uniform, were strolling around the city.

The girls and the sailors got chatting, asking where the others came from in Poland, how the girls got to Palestine, where the sailors were based and where their duties had taken them to.

One of the sailors explained that unusual for sailors in the Polish Navy, he was a survivor of the deportations to Siberia. He explained that he had lost his mother, didn't know if his sisters were still alive, and if they were, where they might be now. As all the girls had been through similar experiences, they started to ask him more questions.

One girl asked him his name.

He said "Jan Stepek".

Another girl said, "What are your sisters' names?"

"Zosia and Danka."

"Zosia and Danka? My God, I think they're here. They're here. They stay with us at our camp."

Jan told the girls to wait for him and ran back to his ship. He recounted the conversation to his Captain who granted him permission to go with the girls to see if it was possible that the girls were right about Jan's sisters.

Jan found Zosia studying at her school desk in one of the classrooms; then together they went to visit Danka who was in a hospital ward suffering from one of her frequent episodes of low blood pressure, fainting and deeper loss of consciousness. Jan and Zosia entered the room, which was long and narrow, a row of beds at either side. Sick girls lay in every bed. From one Danka propped herself up, feeling groggy and her eyes not quite focussed.

"I felt like I was having a dream. My big brother, who I thought might be dead, was walking towards me with my sister, hand in hand. It was such an emotional event. Even all the other sick girls were crying."

The last time the three had been together Jan was not expected to survive his malaria. He was shrivelled and skeletal wearing only rags. Now he looked fit and healthy, dressed immaculately in Polish Navy uniform. It was the smartest dressed they had ever seen their brother in their lives, making the contrast with their past experiences all the greater. It felt like a symbol of hope for all three.

More than this, they had now found each other and from that moment would remain in contact for the rest of their lives, sending each other letters and photographs during the rest of the war years.

As Danka settled into the resumption of her education, Zosia's brief military career came to a surprising end. General Anders, the head of Polish forces formed from the Siberian survivors, countermanded an earlier order from the Polish Government-in-exile in London. The order, through which Zosia had been conscripted into the army, stated that all Poles on reaching the age of eighteen were to be enlisted in the army. Anders abandoned the policy reasoning that for Poland to flourish as an independent state after the war was won, they would need a highly educated, well trained young population, especially highly educated young women, as so many Polish men had been killed in the war. So Zosia was demobbed from the army and began a higher level of education.

As an eighteen-year-old she was now entitled to receive an income from the Polish armed forces. This was in British currency, fifteen shillings for every ten days of work, with two shillings taxed by the Polish authorities. All Poles in employment, armed forces or civilian, had a percentage of their wages deducted to cover the basic costs of food, accommodation, and education of the four thousand Polish children in Palestine.

Zosia shared her remaining income with Danka, and in turn Danka bought jotters, pencils, soap, and other essentials which the Polish authorities could not afford to supply. The British Government no longer financially supported the Polish Government-in-Exile, so the cash-strapped Poles had to fend for themselves.

Aside from the schools for girls there were three schools for Polish boys in Palestine, including one for Air Force trainees and another for trainee mechanics. Meanwhile Zosia was spotted as an intelligent young woman with good language skills and was trained to speak English to a level at which she in turn could teach Polish officers.

The following school year, 1943-44, Danka passed two years of secondary school. However, illness of the Soviet years did not disappear so quickly, and Danka was frequently ill despite good food, accommodation and medical care in Palestine.

"When you have had dysentery to our extent you never fully recover because your inside organs are damaged. It was so hot there. I was always fainting. I had very low blood pressure and the doctors were forever checking my heart. So many doctors and nurses inspected me in those years. For half a year in 1944 I was constantly in and out of hospital. They were sending me to the Red Cross and other organisations, anywhere that had a bed available."

Danka had just one pair of pyjamas while in Palestine which she wore out whilst she was in hospitals trying to recover her health. Just as Zosia had experienced in Persia, now that Danka had access to ample nutritional food she had a sudden sprouting. She grew six inches in less than a year, but this meant that her pyjamas became ridiculously short for her and the Polish authorities did not have the means to buy her replacement ones, as clothing was severely rationed.

Also in Qastina at this time was Danka's cousin Adam, another of Henryk Ciupka's children. He and a friend took Danka's pyjamas, tore them by grinding them between two stones till the fabric ripped apart, then went to the local officer saying that a dog had mauled poor Danka's pyjamas. The authorities now had no choice, and Danka finally received a new pair of pyjamas, ones which fitted her.

Most of the local Arabs were kind and helpful to their Polish guests but one day some local Palestinian boys stole Danka's sheets and other bedding items. Danka had to pay for replacements out of the money Zosia had given her. But this was the exception, and Danka remembers her years in Palestine as ones of great security, the start of lifelong friendships, and of growing from a skeletal, fearful girl to a beautiful, educated young woman. The local Arabs would gift them grapes as they walked the streets freely, and the girls felt safe enough to hitch lifts to and from towns in British army jeeps.

In 1945, just before the end of the war, Zosia was posted to Alexandria in Egypt where she taught Polish officers how to speak, read and write in English. The following year, after the war had ended, she was relocated with the rest of the Polish forces in North Africa to England.

Danka stayed on in Palestine after the war ended, but in 1947 when in her last year of secondary school her education was again disrupted. Tensions between Jews and Palestinian Arabs escalated in the lead up to the ending of British rule and the implementation of the United Nations' declaration of the new states of Israel and Palestine. The ongoing troubles led to a decision by Polish officials to evacuate all Poles from the two new states. So just as the Arab-Israeli war was beginning in late 1947 Danka found herself on the move again, this time on a ship that set sail to Liverpool, England.

Part 4 Beginnings

Jan in the Navy Part 1

March to July 1943

Jan was still weak when he arrived in Basra to rejoin his army unit. For a few days his health improved but then he was struck by yet another disease. Although he slowly recovered over the following days he determined to get out of the Middle East and the tropical diseases that seemed to follow him wherever he went. He felt sure that he would not survive another bout, so he was thrilled when a friend told him in early February 1943 that the Polish Navy was seeking recruits from the mass of soldiers now in the Middle East and North Africa.

When the Polish Navy officials came to assess potential recruits, Jan was one of only a handful of soldiers interested in a transfer. Fighting on land had a stronger hold on the imaginations of the soldiers, perhaps for historical reasons; all of Poland's great military victories and legends were on land, and the country had little naval warfare heritage. Still, Jan's reasons for applying were far more urgent and pragmatic – survival and the chance to recover his health.

He felt he had acquitted himself well in the interview, and the officers seemed to like this young twenty year old, thin as a rake and obviously not yet back to full health, but their response was a bombshell.

"We're very sorry but you are too small to join us. We have a minimum height requirement and you have failed it by several centimetres."

Jan's response was instantaneous.

"But surely you have submarines. And in a submarine being short is an advantage, not a problem."

Imagine the officers' reaction. This skinny waif, barely a man yet, trying to out-argue senior Naval officials, and point-blank refusing to take no for an answer. It was very unmilitary; it was disrespectful, verging on arrogant.

I'm sure they suppressed a desire to laugh at this defiant young ball of energy. Ultimately, they had seen so many young men and women die in the past few years that they did not have the heart to refuse this youngster's plea to join the navy, regardless of whatever personal reasons he may have had.

So it was that the young soldier was accepted into the Polish Navy. He was to be a sailor then, despite never having seen an ocean in his short life. Jan Stepek of the Polish 8th Infantry Division since 10th February 1942, was on 11th March 1943, officially 30195179 Private / Able Seaman 2 Jan Wladyslaw Stepek.

Things moved fast. Within a matter of days he was taken to the nearest port where there was a ship travelling in the right direction for a new Polish Navy sailor to join his comrades. Which port it was is unknown but most likely would have been somewhere in today's southern Iraq, south-west Iran, or Kuwait.

Jan remembers stopping three times in different ports in Africa, including South Africa, so the once farm boy was now sailing the entire coastline of the continent of Africa then finally they came to their destination: Liverpool, England.

It was a cold, wet and bleak early morning, and as Jan peered out at the gloom he saw dirty, cramped houses and the noise and darkness of heavy industry. And he thought dispiritedly to himself "So this is the great British Empire. This is the force that has dominated the world."

No doubt his mind would have returned to Maczkowce, its rolling hills, its greenery, its farm animals and the rivers and the snow and its fertile soil. What a contrast. What a harsh reality. But he was used to harsh realities now.

If Liverpool was a shock and a surprise, he hadn't long to wait for better experiences. As soon as he disembarked, he was taken on a train northwards, to Glasgow. Almost the entire journey was through lovely scenery - the beauty of the Lancashire countryside, then the Lake District, followed by the Scottish Borders with its beautiful austere hills. Glasgow returned him to the frenetic and dirty realities of Britain as the workshop of the world, but he had little time to dwell on such things as he was taken to a second train.

This train was busy, with mostly local people but they seemed to be speaking a completely different language from the little English Jan had heard from the American, English, and Indian doctors and nurses in hospital in Persia. Glaswegian, he quickly realised, was a tongue of its own.

And if he thought that was challenging he had more in store. The train stopped at Kirkcaldy, in Fife. Jan, staring at the name, couldn't even begin to understand why people were taking about somewhere called Kirkody. He saw the sign and pronounced it Kirktsaldy. This would not be the last time the young Pole had trouble with Scottish place names.

It was 1st March 1943. He was taken by truck to the Polish Army's training camp in Kinghorn, Fife for medical tests and basic training for a week before being sent back down to England to formally join the Navy, which he did on 11th March.

The Polish Navy was headquartered in Plymouth so Jan and his new colleagues lived in camps then in nearby barracks for the next few weeks. Jan was allocated to the ORP (abbreviation for Ship of the Polish Republic) Krakowiak, a destroyer, which had already been involved in wartime action in the Mediterranean. The ship had returned to Britain in the early part of June 1943 and Jan was on board when it set sail again on June 23 as part of the Mediterranean fleet.

Much of his time was spent doing mundane tasks such as sweeping the decks and maintaining basic machinery and weaponry. What he most recalls of his early days on board was more basic yet; seasickness and vomiting every single day for the first month at sea.

Soon he had bigger things to worry about. The Krakowiak was involved in Operation Husky, the invasion of Sicily in late June and early July 1943. This was part of the Allies' grand strategy to retake parts of Europe from the south while preparing for the Normandy Landings the following year.

It was Jan's first real taste of war despite having been its victim for almost four years. He didn't feel any excitement about battle, nor a sense of finally being able to avenge Poland or even his mother's death. His view was that he had no choice but to serve, he was on a battleship, and now it was going to shell and be shelled. Completely fatalistic at the time, in retrospect he did consider this attitude as neither patriotic nor professional, but accepted that this was just how he was at the time. Occasionally he could be insubordinate to officers, questioning why he was chosen to do a particular task, or querying decisions by raising other suggestions.

He saw death again, but in a different sphere and in a very different way. German ships intercepted the fleet and a battle broke out. The Allied fleet was much stronger than the German and soon Jan could see several German ships on fire and sinking close to where he stood on deck. One of the stricken ships was close enough for Jan to hear the shrieks and cries of the German sailors burning to death. He could see bodies scattered in the water. Some were living, desperately swimming for their lives. Others floated on the surface, having experienced death by drowning, still others a burned-out corpse.

After the battle Jan was engaged in helping the survivors. As he helped pull desperate sailors onto the ship any sense of hatred towards the Germans vanished. They were just ordinary people, like him. War was insane, he thought, but there was nothing he could do about that.

Having done their part in the successful invasion of Sicily, the Krakowiak and its crew left the battle scenes, ferrying other Allied ships' survivors and German prisoners. They sailed towards Haifa, in British-occupied Palestine, for refuelling and restocking of necessities before their next operation.

At this moment in his life Jan is still only twenty years old. He is alone in the world, having lost his mother, not knowing if his father - already frail before the war started - is dead or alive, and aware that his two sisters had not fully recovered their health. He hopes they are still secure in Persia. He hopes that deep frailty and disease had not taken them from him.

Death on land. Death in the sea. It is in his memory. It is in his heart. He has an overwhelming feeling that he is a pawn in a gigantic game and determines to do anything he can to survive within this hugely oppressive paradigm. Nothing more, just survive. Moment by moment, day by day, wherever it leads.

In Haifa, as we have already seen, he found a rare, precious joy which was to stay with him for seventy more years.

Jan in the Navy Part 2 August 1943 to 1946

Jan's elation at finding his two sisters, alive if not in full health, lasted a lifetime, but his time with them in Palestine was short-lived. Within twenty-four hours he was back on board and sailing towards Italy and the campaign to defeat that country.

In this time Jan's life became typical of all who serve in the armed forces during wartime - long stretches of dull, monotonous work and periods of doing nothing, interspersed with horrific episodes of death and destruction. The ORP Krakowiak played its part in the campaigns for the invasion of Italy and the liberation of the Cyclades and Dodecanese islands of Greece in November 1943. Jan remembered particularly the liberation of the island of Samos from the Italian forces, and some months later experienced a deep spasm of sadness when he heard the news that the island had been retaken, this time by the Germans.

The ship docked in Alexandria on the first of December and while awaiting news of the next operation the crew were allowed shore leave. Many accepted the opportunity to visit the Great Pyramid and the Sphinx, where photographs were taken to capture the surreal image of Polish sailors site-seeing in the midst of a global conflict. How Jan must have felt about this we don't know, but he must have thought that only five years earlier he had been a farm boy, hoping to see his family at Christmas, and now, still only twenty-one years old, he was in Egypt staring at the one remaining wonder of the seven wonders of the ancient world.

Soon after, the ship set sail again and Jan spent that Christmas docked in Gibraltar. The New Year brought further campaigns as the Allies sought to maintain their growing grip on southern Europe and to press northwards through Italy. Jan found himself returning to Gibraltar in March 1944 then later that same month he stepped foot on Italian soil for the first time in his life, at Naples. Soon after the ship docked in Oran, Algeria.

By May he was back in England, the Krakowiak having docked in Portsmouth. Unknown to Jan and his colleagues their officers were now waiting on news of their next operation, which was to be one of the defining actions of the war. As part of this, towards the end of May, Jan was seconded to another destroyer, the ORP Slazak.

On the night of 5-6 June 1944, Danka, in bed in Palestine, had a premonition that Jan was in terrible danger. Unknown to her the Slazak had just set sail with hundreds of other Allied ships. By morning they were shelling the beaches of the Normandy coast. D-Day had commenced.

Following the invasion of France, Jan's life revolved around repeated journeys across the English Channel to bring further personnel and supplies for the final push through Western

Europe towards Germany. There were no major military incidents experienced by Jan during this period. However, Jan's mental health suffered a prolonged collapse. Perhaps it was the absence of major incidents to keep his mind distracted from his feelings, that allowed his body time to finally feel the enormity of all that he had been through. Whatever the reason he was hospitalised or sent to what his war records say was a "rest home" five times in a five month period between November 27 1944 and April 30 1945. In between times however he trained and qualified as a radar operator in February of that year.

Then just as he recovered, the war ended. On 8 May 1945 he was one of millions of Europeans to rejoice when he heard the news that the Germans had unconditionally surrendered. This was tempered by the knowledge that the British and American governments, without consulting the Polish Government, had agreed to the Soviet Union's annexation of Eastern Poland and that Poland would be under Stalin's "sphere of influence" post-war.

To Jan this meant that the home he was born and brought up in was no longer in Poland, but part of the Soviet Union, and that his homeland was occupied by the country which had taken him and his family to Siberia, leading to the loss of his mother. It was a hard reality for a young man, still only 22, and for his younger sisters.

On 27 May the Slazak docked at the occupied German port of Wilhelmshaven on the Baltic Sea. Jan felt it was the hollowest of symbolic victories for him, a Polish sailor, to be walking on the territory of the country which had brought about this cataclysm. Everything seemed ruined. The German city, the bankrupt British Empire, most of Central and Eastern Europe, liberated from the Germans but now under Stalin's control, and of course most of all, the decimation of his own country and the tragedy of his family's last six years.

Worse news came soon enough. Zosia telegraphed Jan to tell him she had heard from their two Stepek aunts that Wladyslaw had died almost three years earlier, of cancer, in September 1943. In despair Jan broke the sad news to Danka,

"Father is dead. There is nothing to go home to."

On 12 June the Slazak returned to port in England and Jan was officially posted to the Polish Naval Camp in Okehampton, named ORP Baltyk in honour of a ship by that name. Here he was involved in on-shore post-war clean-up operations, including eleven days when he rejoined the Slazak as radar operator for cross-Channel activities, from 7-18 January 1946. He was in limbo, stuck in his military role; a pawn like millions of others serving in the armed forces around the world, waiting to find out what, if anything, he could do to further his life once things settled into a new peacetime normality.

Jan Stepek Part 1: Gulag to Glasgow

New Lives, New Families:

1946 to 1949

Jan's uncertainty as to the future, and what might happen to the Polish troops now that the war was over, took a turn for the better.

The British Government allowed Polish armed forces to remain in the United Kingdom if they were unwilling to go back to their homeland, now occupied by the Soviet Union. Moreover the troops were included in those eligible for grants to study particular subjects at various colleges and universities across the country.

Jan was desperate to leave the Navy and try to find a new life for himself, whether here in the UK, or perhaps use the country as a steppingstone to better opportunities elsewhere. Already some Polish exiles were making plans to emigrate to Canada, America, or Australia.

Jan's first choice of study was Physics but he was immediately refused on grounds that certain foreign nationals were not allowed to study this subject. It was the era of the Cold War and the nuclear age. Jan had been in the Soviet Union for two and a half years, and no matter the reason for this he was deemed to be potentially a spy who could, in due course, steal the West's nuclear information. Ironically that threat proved to come from members of the English upper-class elite rather than mentally exhausted Poles.

Undaunted, Jan applied for another course and was this time permitted to study radio and television engineering. His experience of working on and maintaining radar systems stood him in very good stead for this. So on 19 January 1946 Jan was seconded from the Polish Navy to the Radio and Television College in Renfrew Street, Glasgow. Almost three years after he first set foot on Scottish soil for army training in Fife, fate had taken him back to this far off corner of Europe, so distant from his home.

Given his recent training and experience of working with and repairing radar systems Jan found the course easy. However it was taught in English, and understanding English, especially the unique Glaswegian dialect which combined Scots language, English, and its own regional vocabulary and pronunciations, is what most troubled him.

On 21 March 1946 his formal status in the armed services changed from the Polish Navy to the Polish Resettlement Corps, the title given to all Poles who remained in the United Kingdom. Many of the Poles who remained in Britain were allocated to army barracks while the long, complex and enormous process of rehabilitating people was undertaken. This included not only the Poles and other foreign troops based in Britain during the war, but also millions of British armed forces still abroad.

The country itself was struggling to recover from an arduous and destructive war so Jan was one of a fortunate minority of Poles to have something practical to focus on in his studies, with the real prospect of being able to earn a living using his newly-honed skills.

Jan recalls that the local people of Glasgow were remarkably kind and helpful to the Poles who started to settle down in the city. A woman's group organised day trips for the new refugees; to Loch Lomond, or "doon the watter" to the beautiful Ayrshire seaside resorts of Ayr, Largs and Girvan.

It was not easy for the Poles to forget all they had suffered and lost, but Jan was determined that the past was a world that had now disappeared. If he was to have a full life he must work on making a go of it here in this new land.

One day a Scottish student friend of Jan's persuaded him to go to one of the local dance halls for which Glasgow was famous. There his friend met a local girl whom he knew from his school days and introduced her to Jan. Jan did what he was trained to do at school when meeting a lady; he bowed, clicked his heels, took the young woman's hand, and kissed the back of it.

"Jan Stepek, Miss" he said.

Teresa Murphy was dumbstruck. Glasgow boys did not do introductions like that. This was, well, very strange. Quite nice. Very nice actually. But she wasn't sure whether she should like it or not, whether she should like him or not.

Teresa was only 19 but she had a very practical and realistic mind. How did these foreigners behave with girls, she wondered. Still, he was very striking looking, totally different from the local boys, handsome in a strange way, and very dignified, serious, earnest.

Teresa Murphy knew some hard facts about life. She was born in 1928 to a mining family of Irish descent in Cambuslang, Lanarkshire. Her father died when she was eight, leaving her mother to bring up eleven children through the Great Depression and World War Two on a miner's widow's pension. She supplemented her meagre income by knitting and selling Paisley Pattern shawls and tea cosies at the Barras, the bustling working-class market in Glasgow's impoverished East End.

When she was twelve, and just about to finish primary school, Teresa fell ill with septicaemia from a contaminated needle during a routine school inoculation programme. Her condition worsened rapidly and the doctor told her mother to expect the worst. However, she survived, though for two years Teresa was in and out of hospitals, and was not well enough to return to school during this period. When she finally recovered and was given the option of returning to her studies or leaving school she opted to find a job to bring more much-needed money into the family. It was a tremendous sacrifice for a young teenager, particularly as she had seen the astonishing achievements of three of her elder siblings as they went to Glasgow University and graduated through the nineteen-forties. For a mining family to have a child go to university was rare. For three to reach such heights was near miraculous. For a widowed mother to guide one's children to achieve this through the grimmest of economic and war times... words fail. And young Teresa consciously sacrificed this opportunity for herself in order to help her mother and the whole family.

Teresa was taken on as an apprentice book-keeper, and, studying every evening at a local college, she obtained qualifications in accounting and finance. So by the time she met Jan Stepek at the dance hall she had had five years' experience of life in business.

As for her views on Jan, she wasn't sure.

Jan was sure. He was smitten. Teresa Murphy was the first girl, no, woman, he had ever felt attracted to. Just when his hormones should have been guiding him in that direction the war wiped away any sense of romantic or sexual attraction and replaced it with horror and grief and battles and survival and disorientation. He was finally in a safe country, studying hard, learning a trade, and looking to find a job. Now without even trying he had met the most beautiful young woman he could imagine.

In his clumsy way, hindered by poor English, he tried to woo Teresa. Teresa was irritated by his continual requests for a dance, a date, a chance to walk together along the River Clyde. Didn't he know she was working full-time - and studying at night too? When was she going to have time to go out with anyone, let alone a nuisance like him?

But eventually Jan wore down her resistance and they started dating. When Teresa first took Jan to her family home, her mother asked Jan directly within a few minutes whether he went to mass every Sunday.

"Most Sundays" Jan replied honestly.

She looked at him quite harshly but relented.

"Fine" she said. He was acceptable.

Some months later Jan managed to find a job, in far-off Arbroath. He had to stay there in rented accommodation through the working week, only returning to see Teresa at weekends. As is often the case, it was during this period of enforced absence that their love for one another grew.

After a year's courtship he asked her to marry him, to which she replied, only when he had a local job and earned over five shillings a week. Teresa was already on more than ten shillings. She wanted to be sure they could have a real life together and would be able to rent a home of their own without worrying about paying the bills. And of course, before anything could be decided he had to ask permission of her mother, the quiet, tiny but formidable Mrs. Mary Ann Murphy.

Teresa's mother had no objections. She had come to admire the honesty of the young man, his dedication to Teresa and his obvious desire to make a go at being successful in life.

During the same period Jan was formally Honourably Discharged from the Polish Armed Forces. The date, 6 August 1948. Six months later on 26 February 1949 Jan Wladyslaw Stepek, by now twenty-six years old married the twenty-year old Teresa Murphy.

Danka and Zosia were both now in England, and had taken first steps forward in their lives in this new land.

Danka finished her last year of secondary school in 1948, sitting exams just before her twenty-first birthday. Nine years after it was interrupted by war, she had completed her education. She had also found a young Polish man, Hubert Bienkowski. They quickly fell for each other and married.

Zosia qualified as a teacher of English under the English education system and started a long career in that profession in the south-east of England. She met a Polish ex-army officer, Jozef Repa, and they married in Paris within a year of meeting.

Thus before a decade had passed since their deportations to Northern Russia on February 10 1940, the three young Stepek siblings had tentatively established new lives in Great Britain, married, and began a new phase of what was to prove to be very long lives. They had, each in their own way, found a way to internalise and manage the experiences and memories of terror, illness, bereavement and malnutrition, and now entered a new, more secure stage in their lives. But it was to be a life bereft of mother, father, home, and Poland, their homeland.

Postscript

As I write this, on 21 March 2024, my father Jan Stepek has been dead for over ten years, having died one month after his ninetieth birthday on 26 October 2012. Zofia died in January 2017 at the age of ninety-one, and their younger sister, Maria Danuta, my Aunt Danka, passed away in November 2019. She was ninety-two years old.

It beggars belief that they lived such long lives, and I feel blessed for having known them, though sadly I only knew Zosia a very little, London seemingly a long arduous trip for someone living in Central Scotland. That I regret.

Each of their lives in post-war Britain deserve a book of their own but I have spent twenty years on-and-off pulling together this one and my next aim is to focus on writing a book on my father's life in Scotland.

Jan became a highly successful businessman, and thanks to a twenty-year television and radio advertising campaign, the obscure Polish surname Stepek became a household name in Central Scotland. Equally important in his life was his philanthropy to local charities, and his active support of the cause for a free and democratic Poland. Jan became a long-serving chairman of the football club, Hamilton Academical, saving them from extinction and the newspaper headline "Is this the worst team in Britain?" and later attaining promotion to the top division in Scottish football.

Looking back, the epic tragedy of their lives between 1939 and 1947 is hard to put into words. At a raw visceral level, I grieve for my grandmother and grandfather, and for the absence of them in my own life. I miss my father but cannot see the teenage Jan in the father I knew. I never saw my father threatened. I never knew how he related to his sisters or his parents, only how he related to me, my brothers and sisters, and my mother. He was a force of nature, resonating action and decisiveness.

The boy-man he was in 1939 and the man-boy who was demobbed in 1946, I feel for him. I think he lost so much, had to battle the losses, had to suppress his grief, his multiple griefs, in order just to survive. What he thought when he saw his mother malnourished, swollen to the chest. What he felt when he saw his little sisters slowly become skeletal and weak. I think it must be like those occasions when the body loses consciousness because the physical pain is too great to bear. He lost something so great in those years that I think it was only in the years leading up to his death that little gaps appeared in the otherwise impermeable front. Then, in brief moments the tears would come. When we got together as a family to celebrate his and mum's sixtieth wedding anniversary in 2009 he cried when he said how much he owed to mum. Tears, I think, that he had held back for almost seventy years. He cried more after that, not frequently, but not just occasionally, and they were healthy tears. He once said he wished he had spent more time with us, his kids. I wish he had been able to let the dam burst, let the whole unbearable flow of pain and loss wash over us all, his family, drowning us in a better understanding of the magnitude of his loss and his strength.

The same is probably true for Zosia and Danka, though I can't speak so clearly of them as I can for my dad.

I think of refugees. Syria. Libya. Somalia. Yemen. Afghanistan. Myanmar. All these peoples, brutalised, traumatised, seeking asylum in a new land. Seeking security, safety, peace. Seeking a chance of a new life.

In a different part of my working life I teach people how to know peace. How to let go. How to accept what is and what was. How to enjoy life for the wonder and miracle it is despite all the suffering.

Everyone who has suffered wants peace. Just peace, respite, the pain to stop. I know peace. I am the grateful recipient of its beauty. I would have loved to bring peace to my father and his sisters, and to my grandparents but that's not how it turned out, so I accept. But if I can bring a measure of peace to others then in a way, through the beauty of creativity, I can imagine that that work reaches through death and distance and goes deeply into my lost loved ones and affords them a posthumous peace. But how stupid. Death brought them peace. They don't need my counsel. It's me who needs to find peace through accepting the loss of such remarkable people from my life. In many ways the writing of this book is my way of letting go of the grief I have deep inside me for the five people as they were between 1939 and 1943.

Finally, this is my Polish heritage, unspoken and unrecorded for many decades. Now it is recorded, chiselled in stone as it were, to capture in words that these people existed and had these epic experiences, to say, these things happened.

Acknowledgements

I have worked on this memoir of my father and his family for twenty years, on and off in my alleged spare time. Many people and organisations have helped me en route. Two global community research charities, Kresy-Siberia and Kresy-Family, helped me find important information and details in the early years of the internet, about the Poles deported to the Soviet Union during the Second World War.

Two strangers from Haczow, now friends, did research there for me on my family history, especially about my grandfather's remarkable heroics during the First World War. So a huge thanks to Krzysztof Golab and Witek Blaz.

I'd like to thank my oft-time publisher, Etta Dunn, of Fleming Publications, who was going to publish this book. However a series of challenges mean this couldn't be the case and I took over the reins.

To my own family, who put up with me endlessly repeating stories I had already told them, and who learned not to push me too hard when the book, yet again, didn't appear when I told them it would, over a period of many years.

Most importantly to my late father, Jan Stepek, and his wonderful sisters, my aunts Zofia and Maria Danuta, who warmly shared with me the joys of their early years and the traumas that followed, and their recollections of their parents, my grandparents, whom I was fated never to know.

Finally to three people dear to me but no longer with us and so will never read this book: my brothers David and John, and my sister Maria. I love and miss you. I am sorry that I wasn't able to get this finished and published before you left us. This book is dedicated to your memory.

Martin Stepek

March 2024

Printed in Great Britain
by Amazon

48534046R00145